SEX AND THE SINGLE PERSON

BY DR. BARBARA JOHN

Copyright © 2004 by Dr. Barbara John

Sex And The Single Person
by Dr. Barbara John

Printed in the United States of America

ISBN 1-594674-91-4

All rights reserved solely by the author. The author guarantees all contents are original and do not infringe upon the legal rights of any other person or work. No part of this book may be reproduced in any form without the permission of the author. The views expressed in this book are not necessarily those of the publisher.

Unless otherwise indicated, Bible quotations are taken from the Application Study Bible, NLT Version. Copyright © 1996 by Tyndale House Publishers.

www.xulonpress.com

CONTENTS

Acknowledgements vii
Introduction ix

1. Sex 13
2. Sex Is Good And Of The Lord 17
3. Virginity 21
4. Secondary Virginity 29
5. Abstinence and Chastity 33
6. Dating 37
7. When One Is Looking For A Life Partner 43
   i. Who Should Marry 50
   ii. Choosing The Right Partner 55
8. Sexual Sin? 57
   i. Sex Before Marriage 65
   ii. Stimulating One's Self (Masturbation) 67
   iii. Single Persons Co-habiting Together
        (Common Law Marriage) 69
   iv. An Alternative Life Style 74
9. Dealing With One's Sexuality 77
10. Sexual Instinct 83
11. The Uniqueness of Both Sexes 87
12. The Answer 91
    i. By a Life of Prayer 92
    ii. By Reading God's Word Daily 95
    iii. Keep Busy, Especially Busy in the Service
         of God 98
    iv. Focus on the Promises that God Made to Us, Both
        Personally and through His Word 99

    v. Remember all the Promises and Commitment that We in turn have made to Him 100
    vi. Think of God's Love for us, and our Love for Him 101
13. The Joy of Being Single 103
14. The Song of Solomon 107
15. Commitment Abstinence Pledge 117
16. References 119

ACKNOWLEDGEMENTS

I would like to thank two very special ladies who have made an indelible impression on my life, my mother, Clariena John and my pastor, Rev. Margaret Lee. They have always encouraged me to strive for excellence. I would also like to thank all those persons who contributed and assisted me in any way with the compilation of this book. I love you all.

INTRODUCTION

I decided to write this book because I realized through my own experience of becoming a single person and interacting with other single people, that there is a dire need for education on the subject of sex and the normal sexual desires that single people experience. This book has the answer to some practical ways whereby persons can have victory over their sexual desires thereby living happy and godly lives.

When I look at our present system of education, I realize with great sadness, that there are not enough measures in place in most schools to deal with the spiritual and social issues that affect young people in our society. In some schools, the Bible and Christ have no place and children are not encouraged to pray, as they should.

I have been saved for about seventeen years and have been single seven out of these seventeen years. In all this time not much has been said on the sanctity of being single and the spiritual significance of keeping oneself pure before the Lord. One is simply told not to be **"unequally yoked"** and **"flee fornication and adultery."**

However I never thought much about this subject until I myself became single and had to deal with some serious issues in relation to my own sexuality. It was one of the most difficult situations that I have ever had to deal with, hence the reason for this book. A significant amount of the church population is made up of single persons, and yet not much attention is given to them in relation to how they need to deal with their sexual desires when they arise.

The Bible states that the flesh is weak and desperately wicked. Just telling single persons not to fornicate would not solve it. There has to be practical ways and guidelines whereby this emotion or "problem" can be addressed and dealt with effectively. No matter who you are, whether married or unmarried, sexual feelings will arise and it is time that we as Christians address and deal with this situation and not deny or sweep it under the carpet, (as people did long ago) and call it ungodly.

Sex is a part of life created by God and the only time that God sanctions and permits sex is within the bounds of marriage, anything outside of this is **sin**.

Psalm 1 depicts the perfect walk of a Christian, and this psalm should be indelibly implanted in the hearts and minds of Christians, especially single Christian believers in order for them to live a holy and godly life pleasing to God.

Hence,

Psalm: 1

"Blessed is the man that walketh not in the counsel of the ungodly, nor standeth in the way of sinners, nor sitteth in the seat of the scornful.vr.1

But his delight is in the law of the Lord, vr.2

and in his law doth he meditate day and night. And he shall be like a tree planted by the rivers of waters, that bringeth forth his fruit in his season; his leaf also shall not

wither; and whatsoever he doeth shall prosper. vr.3
The ungodly are not so: vr.4 but are like the chaff which the wind driveth away. Therefore the ungodly shall not stand in judgement, nor sinners in the congregation of the righteous. vr.5
For the Lord knoweth the way of the righteous: but the way of the ungodly shall perish." vr.6 (KJV)

This psalm depicts and explains exactly the manner and lifestyle that is expected of children of the most high God, and the blessings that can be accrued when our lives line up with the Word of God. Also, the consequences that can be incurred when one goes contrary to the Word of God, neglecting His commandments and yields him or herself to the arm of the flesh. Each day, as single people, one should without fail, offer up one's self and one's sexuality unto the Lord. It is only when one is in His hands that one can be truly kept.

SEX

Sex is a subject that is hardly discussed in the Church of Jesus Christ, but is very much in the thoughts and minds of both men and women. It spans all ages and socio-economic barriers from the young to the not so young, and the rich to the poor. Whether one is a Christian or not, sex still remains the same and plays a very important and integral part in the lives of men and women worldwide.

It is a subject that should not be pushed under the carpet and hidden as a dirty secret, because it is not. There is a very great need for everyone, especially believers to be enlightened about it. Situations concerning this subject will most definitely present itself in a person's every day life, and as young believers we need to equip ourselves in order to deal with these feelings when they present themselves. This should be done according to God's Word.

The Oxford English Dictionary defines sex as 'being male or female', however, the world and society refers to sexual intercourse as sex and so would I in this book, the correct term being copulation. **The dictionary also defines sexual as 'mutual attraction of two individuals of opposite sexes'.**

Sex is pure and it is from the Lord, but it is this very

same pure thing that Satan tries to pollute by enticing a person to engage in outside the bounds of marriage. God intended the sexual act to be the means by which the human race is propagated. However, it is one of the most unique and enjoyable things that a person can engage in.

God formulated the sexual act in such a way that it is very pleasurable and brings great delight and satisfaction to both the male and his female partner. Note, I stated the male and his female partner, not female and female or male and male, because when God created man, He made them male and female.

Gen.2: 18, 21-25 relates the plan of God: -

> *"And the Lord God said, "It isn't good for man to be alone; I will make a companion for him, a helper suited to his needs." Then the Lord God caused the man to fall into a deep sleep, and took one of his ribs and closed up the place from which he had removed it. and made the rib into a woman, and brought her to the man. This is it!" Adam exclaimed. "She is part of my own bone and flesh! Her name is 'woman' because she was taken out of a man. This explains why a man leaves his father and mother and is joined to his wife in such a way that the two become one person. Now although the man and his wife were both naked, neither of them was embarrassed or ashamed."* (TLB)

We were made in the image and likeness of God. Man's sexual drive is an instinctive God given part of his human nature, which is meant however to be controlled by man himself. The word "man" in this instance is used in the generic sense and is used to refer to man (male) and woman (female). The same rules applying to both. Man (male), is not permitted to enjoy greater liberty in the expression of his sexual instinct than his female counterpart.

SEX IS GOOD AND OF THE LORD

Sex is not a hidden subject in the Bible. Because the Bible clearly and repeatedly speaks out against the misuse or abuse of sex, labeling it "adultery" or "fornication". Many people have misinterpreted the teachings and concluded that God condemns all sex, and when it does take place, it is to be endured. It is only when sex is engaged in outside of the bond of matrimony, that God does not sanction it.

Human sexuality is a most wonderful part of God's creation of man. We are all made in the image and likeness of God. In Gen.2.25 Adam and Eve's original holiness is described as unashamed nakedness. One can clearly gather that sexual desires, as part of God's creation, are not to be considered sinful, bad, or dirty. God created human sexuality and it is a powerful and mysterious force. Sexual desire is one of the strongest desires that God created, but when Adam and Eve fell into sin, God's beautiful creation became marred. Their beautiful sexual powers were subjected to and dominated by sin. When dominated by sin, the sexual desires, which God created, become the "lust of the flesh" (Rom.13.14;). As a result, sexuality, while in itself is good, is often expressed in perverseness.

Man's fall into sin distorted the sexual desires God had created; God redeemed those desires from shame. God reserved them for the wonderful use within the union of marriage and especially for those who marry "in the Lord".

God's redemption of sexual desires means that He is as much Lord of them as He is of everything else. The Bible teaches that sex is a gift of God, a good gift. This gift, enjoyed within the bond of marriage is not selfish or merely romantic, but fulfilling and pleasurable.

Nearly every book in the Bible contains something about it. Two books in the Old Testament have sexual relationships as their theme. God thinks sex is important, and the Scriptures contains numerous guidelines for its use and warns about its misuse. Sex is always mentioned in the context of a loving relationship between a husband and wife.

The Book of Song of Solomon gives details of the love relationship experienced between The Shulammite woman, which symbolizes The Church, and her King Groom - The Lord. I have added a portion of the book of the Song of Solomon at the end of this book, authenticating that God does sanction sex and it is beautiful in His eyes. Proverbs on the other hand explains and warns young persons, especially young men about promiscuity and the error of getting caught in its evil web which can only lead to eventual physical as well as spiritual death. The Bible is not negative on sex, just negative concerning the misuse of it. The negativeness is only present to guide one into a more positive, intimate relationship with Christ (the Bridegroom) and the Church (the Bride).

The Scriptures are the only standard by which we should set our behavior. Sometimes the church avoids the subject of sex and some families skip the book of the Song of Solomon in their devotions because it is thought to be too embarrassing. However, God's treatment of this subject is open and the church must be just as open. To be faithful to

God's Word, the Christian and the church must give due attention to this subject.

Extremists run rampant on every subject and sex is of no exception. On one hand one can believe and hold the view of puritanical philosophy, which adhere that love relationship is fine, but sex is only for the purpose of procreation. On the other hand, one may encounter the "Playboy" philosophy – those who want the freedom to "enjoy sex with whomever they choose." Both views are very wrong. The love relationship is bound by marital commitment, but if it is devoid of sexual pleasure then that too is also wrong. The best and most enjoyable relationship consists of both marital bonds of love and pleasurable sex.

One of the reasons that God designed sex was for the procreation of the human race. In Genesis 1:28, God told Adam and Eve to *"be fruitful, multiply and replenish the earth"*(KJV). In Genesis 2:18 God also said, *"It is not good that man should be alone; I will make an help meet for him."* (KJV) Here one can see another reason, and this was for the complementing of man - male and female. God gave Adam a companion, who later became his wife. She was his helpmate and complemented him. She was also his companion before she became his wife.

VIRGINITY

Virginity is part of the uniqueness which God endowed both men and women in creation, and is a glory to both the man and the woman. God expect both parties, male and female to be virgins at the time of their marriage – not just the women as is customary, because God has no double standards. God still expects His people to respond to the covenant He has provided for them with the fear of the Lord in their hearts. God's standard for virginity before marriage was for a divine purpose. Men and women need to understand the truth concerning virginity. In the biblical light, God holds the fathers responsible for their virginal daughters.

The Oxford English Dictionary defines a virgin as 'a person especially a woman who has had no sexual intercourse.' Virginity also in the dictionary is described as 'modesty, undefiled, spotless, not used or tried.' The commonly used definition for a virgin is someone who has not had sex with a member of the opposite sex. Virginity was and still is a concept that holds serious significance with respect to women.

In this day and age, virginity is regarded as useless by many in the medical profession, as a shame to those with it, as a trophy to be won by "macho men", as an embarrassment to young ladies, and as a nuisance to incestuous parents. Television, movies and romance novels make virginity cheap and it is sacrificed on the altar of "fun". Young girls exchange their virginity for love, in the hope that this will solidify their relationship. Some use it to get love, especially girls who have sexual intercourse with their boyfriends in order to keep them. Some boys use it to feel a sense of inclusion with their peer group. No matter the reason, the consequences are most disastrous. These trends signify society's irreverence and disregard for the rewards of chastity.

God has made man in such a way that at puberty there is an inherent awareness in both male and female about themselves and their sexuality. This is where parents, the church, guardians, caregivers and schools should come in and educate young adults about their bodies and the new feelings that they will no doubt be experiencing. Chastity and abstinence should be taught, not safe sex and the distribution of condoms. It is a proven fact that the condom and safe sex has failed.

I was asked sometime ago to counsel a teenage girl who was an inmate of a penal institution for young women. As I visited the young lady I would occasionally speak to the person in charge of the institution and we would exchange ideas. She realized from talking to me that I had very strong views on sexual purity. Because of this she asked me if I would come at some point in time and talk to the young women of the institution about chastity and premarital sex, along with the dangers of contracting sexually transmitted diseases such as Aids.

To my amazement she told me that when guest speakers came and discussed sex education with the young ladies, they did not as a rule tell and discourage the young ladies to refrain from having sex, (Abstinence). Their solution of protecting one's self was in the use of condoms, which was handed out very freely, hence propriety and morality were completely left out. This reflected society's conflict with God's standard of abstinence.

The assumption is perhaps they believe that it was futile to tell the young ladies not to engage in illicit sex, because they believed that they would do it any way. In spite of this outlook, all young women and some older ones too, should be taught about respecting and loving themselves and their bodies. No one should allow his or her body to be used and abused by anyone.

Christian values need to be taught to young people and one of the first things on the agenda should be the sacredness of their virginity. This should be taught foremost in the home and then in the church and in schools. Children should not have to learn and have their first sexual encounter and experience about sex at the back of a school toilet or on the back seat of a car. It is time that children and young adults are taught the value of keeping themselves pure.

If one would truly consider the spiritual importance and implication of virginity then there would be an enormous decrease in the number of persons engaging in premarital sex.

In **Romans 12:1**, Paul writes: -

> ***"I plead with you give your bodies to God. Let them be a living and holy sacrifice – the kind that he will accept. When you think of what he has done for you, is it too much to ask? (NLB)***

This command is reasonable and it does make good sense. Once a man or woman has presented his body to God as a living sacrifice, holy and acceptable unto the Lord which is His reasonable service, then and only then would he or she be able to present themselves to their mates the same way on their wedding night.

The laws of God are broken when a man or a woman

commits fornication. The Bible states, that the individual that does that sin against his or her own body. God intended the coming together of a man and a woman for the first time to be pure in His sight. This is so, because they are joined not only in the physical realm but also in the spiritual realm.

If one is no longer a virgin and have just realized what they have lost and desires to have it back they can. They may not get it back physically, but they sure can mentally, emotionally and spiritually and also live a chaste life pleasing unto God. God can and will restore one's purity if He is asked. This is called Secondary Virginity.

A single person who indulges in fornication has broken and gone against the laws of God. Virginity is a gift that a person first has to give him or herself and then, to her husband or his wife, because it and represents holiness unto God. It is a gift that should be cherished and be very proud of and given as a token of one's love for their mate. It is a gift that says 'I have kept myself for you and you alone, and I am now giving myself to you in the sight of God.' This not only goes for women but men as well.

In some cultures, especially in the Far East the focus is mainly on women. It is more than her sparkling eyes, her radiant smile, or her exhilarating personality that makes a woman a desirable bride. It is instead the presence of the women's hymen, something, which can affect her marriage prospective, her family's reputation, and even her very life. For those women who have lost their virginity, hymenorraphy, which is hymen repair surgery, actually provide escape from grave social persecution.

The Hymen is a pinkish membranous fold of tissue that covers the external vaginal orifice. The biological function of the human hymen is still unclear; scientists hypothesize that it protects the vagina from infection in infants. The social function of the hymen, however, has been and still is a mythical symbol of virginity in many cultures. The spiritual significance is that it signifies the virginal purity of the woman and acts as a seal. However with the female, upon initial penetration of the vagina by the penis before intercourse, the woman's hymen ruptures and bleeds. The image of a bloody sheet is highly celebrated in many cultures because it represents the purity of a woman and the virility of a man.

In these non-Western societies, the virginity of the bride is valued for religious, social and even economic reasons. For example, the Koran, the Islamic holy book, states that the bride must be a virgin. In China, the bride's virginity determines the amount of betrothal gifts. The presence of the hymen is particularly important for families of prestige who want to keep the family lineage non-contaminated. These traditional cultural beliefs demand the "bloody sheet" no matter what. How good it is for us living in the West, that we do not have to go through this trauma. However, God expects us out of love and respect for Him to live a chase life abstaining from, sexual intercourse until we are married.

In the Jewish culture, there was a distinct manner in which newly wed couples were to come together. My mother was born in Tobago, and has told me that similar practices were also practiced there. Also, similar practices were practiced among the East Indian population in Trinidad.

The evidence of the purity of a woman (a bride) was found in her "tokens of virginity" - that is, the presence of blood on the marital bedclothes/bed-sheet/bloody-sheet. The parents of the bride furnished the newly weds with a set of "bed clothes" for the couple's first night of marriage. On their night together if the man brought a charge against his new bride by accusing her of not being a virgin, this charge was not taken lightly. The parents of the bride in turn would obtain the bedclothes that were soiled on that night and spread them before the relevant authorities to give evidence concerning their daughter or guardian's innocence.

If the tokens were found – if they had proof because of the blood on the bedclothes - then it was evidence that the man had lied in an attempt to gain an annulment or even gain financially from it. When he does that he attempts to defraud his new bride and her parents. His charge, if false in the Jewish culture, was a slander against his new bride, which incurred a serious penalty. First, the husband had to pay the parents of the bride a fine for bringing a false charge against their daughter and was denied the right of a divorce or annulment from her. The penalty relating to this incident in some of the other cultures are similar.

I was reading an article in a newspaper recently. The writer wrote about virginity testing in a province in India, and the headline read thus, "<u>Virginity tests torment women in India's Rajasthan</u>". The article mentioned the torture that brides still go through on their wedding night. She is tested with a skein of thread to determine whether she is a virgin or not. However, this kind of testing does not hold because an unbroken hymen is not the only proof of virginity. Some one can be a virgin and because of a fall or per se riding a horse and even the use of tampons can have their hymen stretched or torn. Not every virgin has her hymen in tack.

The report continued to say that it is only by education that women can be truly protected, because terrible things are done to them when they are found "unworthy". The men also take advantage of this situation because they could get the bride's dowry and still have an annulment if they could find their new bride at fault.

In some cultures in Africa, there are traditions that are kept up even in today's society. One of these customs relate to the circumcision of a woman's clitoris. This circumcision is done to their girl children from the age of about three months to about thirteen years. This is reportedly done to alleviate promiscuity in the female. With the removal of the clitoris there is no sexual feelings in that area. Thus, these girls that have been circumcised stand less chance of becoming promiscuous than the girls who were not circumcised. This is now getting international recognition, with the Human Rights Organizations coming in to help eliminate this practice.

In today's society in the western world most young men and women feel excluded, ashamed and embarrassed if they are in their teens and are still virgins. This should not be, they should be proud that they have kept themselves pure no matter if one is a Christian or not. Satan takes the good things that God has created, one of these things being sex, and twists and turns it into something ugly.

However there is a new breed of young people emerging who are not afraid to stand up and declare that they would remain chaste and abstain, keeping their virginity for their husband or wife to be celebrated on their wedding night. It is gift to be given and any young person who has kept himself or herself for when he or she marries should be very proud of this achievement. It is Satan's deception that makes a person feel badly because he has kept himself pure.

Many parents today know that their children are sexually active and condone it, by neglecting to tell them that what they are doing is wrong. In many instances they do so because they do not want to offend them. Such parents stand guilty before God. It is parents God given right to correct their children when they see them going in the wrong direction, it is part of their duty as parents, if not, they will be held accountable. It is better for parents to let their children know the truth about premarital sex before it is too late. If not, they would be the ones that would have to take up the pieces when their children run the risk of contracting Sexually Transmitted Diseases (STD's) or become young mothers or fathers before they are ready.

SECONDARY VIRGINITY

Secondary Virginity is a gift that a person can receive when they have already lost their virginity. All of us have made mistakes and sinned during our lives and were forgiven. All we did was to ask God to forgive us and He did. It is a gift that I myself have received from God, and it is not restricted to myself alone but to all those who may ask it of Him. It means that besides the forgiveness of our sins, He will restore our purity.

Secondary virginity makes a person emotionally and spiritually whole again. God wants to restore our purity. It is a time to change bad habits and heal past wounds. Even the physical consequences of premarital sex can be devastating and life threatening. Some people underestimate the emotional and spiritual effects of sex outside of marriage. Furthermore, the emotional and spiritual effects of sex can be longer lasting and even more severe than the physical repercussions. The groups of persons who can receive this gift are those persons who have engaged in premarital sex (which includes rape and incest victims), who were married and their spouses have died and divorced persons.

All of us have made mistakes and sinned during our life. However, we need to know and believe that God still loves us and will forgive us. Some people unfortunately believe that premarital sexual sin is too much for God to forgive them. However all we just have to do is simply and sincerely ask Him to forgive us. He will not only forgive us, but He will also restore us to that state as if we have never sinned, to that state of purity.

When we receive Jesus into our hearts we become a brand new creation in Christ Jesus and we become just as if we have never sinned. There is hope in Christ, because it is on our behalf He took all the stripes on His back and went all the way to Calvary, that we could be the righteousness in Him. We are so very precious in His sight.

I have a friend who got married a couple of months ago (this was her second marriage). She told me that she felt just like a virgin on her wedding night, and she even experienced the "shedding of blood" to go along with it. She was not the only person to have related this phenomenon to me. God is able to do abundantly above all that we could ever possibly ask or think. We who are all Secondary Virgins have a bright hope to look forward to. What a blessing.

Lovematters.com/startover.htm have five **steps to becoming a Secondary Virgin they are:** -

- Make a firm commitment to save yourself for marriage from now on, and believe you can do it. (Because you can)
- Get away from people, places, things and situations that weaken your self-control.
- Avoid intense hugging, passionate kissing and anything else that leads to lustful thoughts and behaviour.
- Find non-physical ways to show your love and appreciation.
- Remember that anyone can start over. When you focus on commitment and self-discipline, along with

the grace of God, you will be able to control your impulses.

Secondary virginity is a personal decision to abstain from sexual activity, starting today and continuing until the day you get married. It is an opportunity to start over. Your physical virginity may be lost, but virginity is more than just a physical. It is also spiritual and is manifested in the way you look at God, others and yourself.

ABSTINENCE AND CHASTITY

At a glance Abstinence and Chastity seems to mean the same thing, but when one really examine the words closely, one realizes that the two words carry a different meaning. Abstinence is defined in the <u>Oxford English Dictionary</u> as 'Refraining from any pleasure.' It can also be described as saying "No", it is the denying yourself of something that you would like or may be thinking of doing. Examples can be depicted by a person avoiding certain things like sweets before dinner, refusing to watch a particular TV show that you like and even sex before marriage. Abstinence has become more commonly known as simply refraining from having sexual intercourse before marriage.

Chastity is defined in the <u>Oxford English Dictionary</u> as 'Continence, virginity, celibacy, and simplicity of style or taste.' It is a virtue not a habit, and it is freedom from sexual impurities and is God's beautiful design for our sexuality.

Abstinence is a great practice and it is now being widely advocated in relation to Sexually Transmitted Disease (STD's) such as Aids and HIV. As some things change, so some things remain the same. This is one of the teachings that the Bible admonishes us to practice and make a part of our lives. It is one of the valued disciplines that help us to escape the many disastrous consequences of illicit sex.

Abstinence is also encouraged so that one learns delayed gratification which is saving something now, making it more valuable in time to come. When parents teach a child the value of waiting then the child learns the rewards of delayed gratification.

When one looks at abstinence, it can be seen why people choose to use this term when encouraging young people to save sex for marriage only. However, it is not the best way to understand God's plan for marriage and the gift of our sexuality. Abstinence has certain limitations. This is where Chastity comes in.

Chastity is the virtue of understanding and respecting sex to such a great degree that one keeps it in the appropriate time and place (marriage). We know that God created sex, and everything God created is very good. It entails everyone and it is a lifestyle choice. It means that you understand the power of sex enough to keep it within the bond of marriage.

In our society, many young people think that they are just fine as long as they do not go 'all the way'. Abstinence, from many sources, says, 'don't do it', and avoid 'it' especially while dating. Chastity is an awesome answer for those who struggle with 'abstinence dating.' Chastity believes it is most loving to not tempt your partner, e.g. foreplay and 'making out' is what occurs and leads up to intercourse. Such behavior should be avoided.

Chastity also calls for freedom from all sexual impurities, especially in the mind and heart. Jesus said in Math.5: 28 "*I tell you that any one that looks at a woman lustfully, has already committed adultery with her in his heart*" Chastity requires that one thinks respectfully about members of the opposite sex. True virtue begins in the mind, and actions flow from virtue. Charity calls every heart to desire purity in order to experience true love and respect. God always wants to keep all of His children close to His heart and His love. Impurities, of any kind, will lead or distract Christians from Christ and their faith.

Chastity gives one the freedom to: -

- Break off all unhealthy relationships.
- Date without fear of being propositioned.
- Avoid all STD's or the possibility of getting pregnant.
- Know that you are loved for yourself and not because of your body.
- Give all of yourself to your spouse when you get married.
- Truly love and respect those whom you date.
- Look forward to a very special honeymoon.

Chastity is God's beautiful design for our sexuality. If you choose chastity, it is a wise and healthy choice and you can experience some of the freedom Jesus referred to in the Bible. However, if you use your freedom to not choose chastity, the consequences you face can be, more often than not, life damaging.

DATING

The practice of dating is of recent origin. It is a development of the past few hundred years in Western culture, which is the reason why the Bible does not mention anything specific about it. However, this should not keep us from using the Bible when discussing dating, for the principles, which must govern our dating are found in it. Dating is the middle stage in the process of finding a suitable mate and comes between a couple being friends and getting engaged.

Dating should ultimately lead to marriage. I would not date someone that I know for sure could not be my future husband and lifelong mate. I recommend that every young person that is thinking of dating follow this practice. I do not mean that you have to marry the first person that you date, but it should be someone that you feel comfortable enough with and which in the long term could lead to marriage.

It is very important to me to make sure that the person that I am dating be aware of my stand about marriage and the seriousness with which I take the marriage vows. I believe that marriage is a lifetime commitment.

Christians dating unbelievers should not be encouraged, it is wiser for a believer to date a believer because it alleviates complication that may arise because of the relationship. It seems a waste of time and emotional energy to go out with someone who you know you should not and could never marry.

As a believer on a date physical contact should not be practiced. This is because sexual urges are natural and when aroused will need to be satisfied and appeased, hence no touching, fondling and kissing on the mouth. Any intimate contact should be discouraged because it could lead to sexual intimacy or sexual intercourse.

Young persons when dating should always go out in groups. This has always been the safest way for the boy and girl to get to know each other, cultivating a friendship that could last a lifetime. It is here interacting with other people that his or her personality, character and their love for God would be able to be tested. Going out on a date is just the first base in a relationship.

If you go out on a date by yourself it is best to stay only in public places where interaction is required, the lighting is good and the ambience is conducive to the formulation of a good healthy relationship. If they respect the boundaries that you have placed, then it is worth it to spend a little more time getting to know that person, their friends and family.

A person, who has waited to give himself or herself to the one that he or she loves and will marry, should not settle for just anyone. He or she should know without a shadow of a doubt that the person that he or she has dated and decide to continue dating and would like to have a further relationship with is worth the wait.

When a Christian man or woman goes out with an unsaved partner, this is just a recipe for trouble, because they are on two different wavelengths, from two different worlds. If by chance they do not kiss on the first few dates, their unsaved partner will eventually demand some form of physical contact. If they go out long enough with the unbeliever, emotional ties will occur, and may eventually fall in love with the person. This may eventually end up with the believer throwing caution to the wind; until he or she gets up one morning only to realize that he or she is no longer a virgin. This is where remorse may step in, along with the many problems that can occur with having unprotected sex.

The last thing a believer may have in their purse or wallet will be a condom, because when the act occurs that person may not have consciously and deliberately decided to have sex. Some women have had the experience of foreplay that began with the external fusing of the male's private part on her body and vagina. This, in almost every instance has led to the complete sex act. One consequence of this being a regrettable unwanted pregnancy.

Dating as a Christian person and dating someone in the world is totally different. The Christian understanding of dating should be different from that of the unbeliever. Dating according to the world's standards is mostly based on the flesh and sexual contact is expected. It is normal for persons to kiss or even go to bed with their partner on their first date.

Some Christian young men try to date as many young ladies in the church as decency would allow. One month they may date one girl, the other month another girl. This should not be. Young ladies, do not let young men use you for their convenience. This practice should not be encouraged in the Body of Jesus Christ. Young ladies if a young man asks you for a date but he does not want you to tell anyone, or does not want to be seen with you, do not bother with that relationship. He is not sincere. If he were he would want it to be known that he is taking you out.

The Bible warns us to resist temptation. That is why it is stressed when you go out with anyone do not go out alone. Therefore young persons are advised to avoid places that are conducive to intimacy – that means that bedrooms are off limit, not leaving room for the enemy of our souls to step in. This is also the breathing ground for date rape to take place. The Bible states that we must not give place to the devil.

A person should not date simply because: -

- Their friends are dating.
- It is good for his/her social status.
- Of financial gain.
- He or she wants to get someone jealous.
- That individual wants to have a boyfriend or girlfriend.

Some unhealthy dating practices can result in: -

- Date rape.
- Premarital sex.
- Lost of self-respect.
- Backsliding
- Depression

Before one thinks of dating, one needs to work on one's personal, intimate, eternal relationship with God. Only when one is secure in Christ can that person enjoy a successful personal, intimate, until-death-do-us-part relationship with another human being. However, this relationship should never be better than the relationship with God.

If you need a husband or wife do not be too bashful to tell God all your desires, because he knows anyway, so you cannot fool Him. Tell Him what you want. I heard a visiting minister say once that even before she met her husband she prayed for him every day, just as if she knew him. When he did come into her life she knew him, and they just clicked together. We should all pray for the partners that God have in store for us, those that we can see and those we cannot see. Even parents need to pray that God would send the right person into their children's lives to be their life partner. This is very important for a successful marriage.

WHEN ONE IS LOOKING FOR A LIFE PARTNER

It is very important when a man or woman is looking for a mate that they find someone that they can cultivate a good healthy relationship and companionship with. Also I might add, one with whom to the best of knowledge would be sexually compatible with. It cannot be emphasized enough that a healthy relationship should be cultivated between one's prospective spouse and himself or herself before marriage. A husband should be his wife's best friend; and vice versa. This attitude produces good communication between husband and wife.

There are single people who keep saying that they would like God to give them a mate. However, if you talk to them for a while what you will hear coming from them is information about their previous boyfriend or girlfriend. When two persons engage in sexual activity before marriage, a bond develops between the two persons that is extremely hard to break. This bond is called a **Soul Tie** and it takes only the grace of God and their renouncing of their past relationship for that tie to be broken.

If a person cannot be a friend or companion to anyone marriage should be forgotten, until they have dealt with that area in their life. However, if one is excited and satisfied with the person, who lives inside their mate's body, then it make all the difference in the world in their attitude towards sexual fulfillment when married. If not, problems would undoubtedly arise somewhere later down in their marriage, and that may ultimately lead to divorce and singleness again if help is not sought.

In marriage the focus must be on the person – not on the sexual performance, but on giving pleasure to one's spouse. Love is not just about receiving but also about giving. John 3:16 states that *"For God so loved the world, that He gave His only beloved son."* When a person truly loves someone, then that person would want to please and give pleasure to the other.

Satan, the enemy of our soul, knows exactly the person that we have a preference for. Every now and then he would bring someone into our lives that we could be attracted to. It may be a tall dark and handsome man or a very beautiful woman. However, if he or she is not interested in Jesus then it is best not to take the relationship further. It may be hard at the time, but it would be worse in the future if the relationship is allowed to continue and blossom.

The Word of God states that He will not give us more than we can bear and Satan the accuser of the brethren always has to get permission from God in order to touch us in any area of our lives. Like Job, God is only setting us up for a blessing, whereby our place of pain becomes our place of gain. God is an awesome God and He cannot use us if we have not gone through the process. So stay focus.

A person who displays a tendency towards having a very high sex drive should never make that the ultimate reason for getting married, it would never last. Each person has a particular area in life that he struggles with. If a person has struggles in any area of his life and in particular his sexuality, then what needs to be done is to submit them to

God, and yield that particular area of his life to Him, in order in bring the flesh under subjection. Nothing else would work in keeping the flesh under subjection but the mighty power of the Holy Ghost. If a person tries to do it in the flesh or in his own strength, it would never work and failure and falling to the ways of the flesh would be his way or life.

I remember in a particular church there arose a problem of that nature. There was this young lady who had a very high sexual drive, and after many counseling sessions with the pastor, he decided the best thing for the young lady to do was to get married, and she did. Not very long after her husband got a new job that entailed him working shift hours, and this started the beginning of their problems. As a result, when her husband worked nights she felt lonely and having a very high sexual drive eventually engaged in extra marital affairs with other men. A problem culminating in the termination of her marriage.

Thanks be to God for making provision for us through His Son Jesus Christ, whereby in Him and through Him we can be victorious over all the works of the flesh. Jesus took all our sin upon Himself when He went to Calvary in order for us to be victorious over every area of our lives.

People should not also desire to get married because their friends are getting married. They do not want to be considered the odd one out so they do every thing in their power to get married. They may also realize that they are getting older and want to get married so desperately that they fall for the first person that pay them a little attention and who may propose to them.

Marriage is very serious and when persons are thinking about getting married, they need to seek God's perfect will for their lives. If they do not, and they eventually get married, it is more than likely that they will not be happy, and will eventually end up being divorced and single once again.

It is important for single persons to seek God's face

when they are contemplating marriage with their prospective spouses. They should not be so anxious to get married that they do not seek the will of God in such situations. If they do they will be alleviated from a tremendous amount of heartache and pain in time to come. I can attest to that in my own marriage. When my ex-husband proposed to me I told him that I did not have any confirmation from God. Nevertheless, I married him because I loved him. He told me that God told him that I should be his wife and there were some prophesies that came forth from persons who knew him saying that God had ordained it. All this time God never told me anything. So my dears, it is better to be forewarned. Do not go by how you feel but make sure from God that that is the person whom He has reserved for you. Have godly counsel, especially from your pastor.

A person should not be so desperate to be married that she accepts the first proposal that she gets, only to find out when they do marry that they do not love one another and still have to endure an intimate relationship with each other. They would be rudely awakened to the fact that real life and sexual intimacy are not what it was portrayed to be in the various movies and soap operas and books that they read.

I know of two young ladies who were members of a church that I attended many years ago. They decided **that they were getting old** (although they were in their twenties, so they decided to 'help God out'. One decided that she would have the best of both worlds because she could not find a good "church boy" attractive enough for her. She started dating "unsaved men", (still coming to church as if nothing happened) until she was exposed when she got pregnant. This young lady had one child and then went on to have another one for a different person. She is now still single after many years, and with two children to maintain and nurture without the help and support of their respective fathers.

The enemy always comes to steal, kill and to destroy, and he does his job well, that is why the Apostle Paul said in Eph. 4:27 *"Give no place to the devil."*(KJV) **Satan is just like a termite**; he just keeps eating and chipping away, taking you down the road towards the path of destruction with the ultimate goal and agenda, death. King Solomon in Proverbs speaks to young men about how they should walk, stressing to them that illicit sexual liaisons can lead to spiritual and physical death.

If a woman, especially a single woman does not respect herself how can she expect a man to respect her? It is of grave importance that women love and respect themselves, knowing and believing that God loves them. Most of the time it is because of this lack of love that she enters into a relationship seeking to find love in someone other than the Lord and ends up being used, abused, ridiculed and then refused.

Christian young ladies are prized target for unsaved young men. It is therefore important that they become aware of their own sexuality so that they will not be fooled and cajoled into doing anything that they know is not right in the sight of God. This goes for single young men as well. In Proverbs 6 and 7 King Solomon admonishes young men to walk holy, avoiding immoral women and sexual sins.

The Bible says in Proverbs 22:6 *"Train up a child in the way they should go: and when he is old, he will not depart from it."* (KJV) If a young person follow the Word of God and seek God's face and His will for his life he would not be led astray, but *"he shall stand like a tree planted by the rivers."* Psalm.1:3 (KJV)

Solomon also addressed women. In proverbs 31 he speaks about the virtuous woman. The woman described in this chapter has outstanding ability; she has strong character, great wisdom, many skills, and great compassion. Some people have the mistaken view that the ideal woman in the Bible is retiring, servile and entirely domestic, however, this is not so, she is a manufacturer, manager, farmer, and seamstress among other things. However her strength and dignity did not come from her amazing achievements, but from her reverence for God. This is an amazing accomplishment for any woman of any era. This is what we, as young women, should ascribe to be like.

> **Proverbs 31:30-31**
> ***Charm is deceptive, and beauty does not last, but a woman who fears the Lord will be greatly praised. Reward her for all she has done. Let her deeds publicly declare her praise.*** (NLT)

Christian ladies, this is the time to make a stand for righteousness. When we stand for righteousness then the Lord has no other choice but to fight our battle for us. He said in His Word *"that when the enemy comes, like a flood the spirit of God would raise up a standard against it." Isaiah 59:19 (KJV)*. For we are more than conquers through Christ who loved us and gave Himself for us.

Young single women should never find themselves becoming involved with married men. There is a single man out there for you. Stand by the Word of God, remind Him of His promise to let every man have his own wife and every wife her own husband 1.Cor.7:2.(KJV) Call your husband from the spiritual realm into the natural or physical realm. Pray for him everyday as you would pray for someone who you can see physically. The spiritual world is just as real than the physical world.

I remember when I was in my early twenties, probably twenty years of age and unsaved at the time, a young gentleman that I knew took me out on a few dates. To my great surprise after a couple of dates I learnt from someone other than himself that he was married. I never accepted another invitation to go out on a date with him after receiving that information. I found out from him years later that his wife had died of cancer not long after I stopped seeing him. However, He is now saved and has never remarried, and we have now become very good friends.

The second young lady that I also previously mentioned, fell in-love with an "unsaved" man because she also felt that there was no man in the church that was suitable or good enough for her. She eventually left the church and backslid for some years and had children for the same man who she said loved her, but he never married her. She eventually returned to church with about four children and still single. The price of disobedience is high. This heartache and pain could have been avoided. Believe God for a godly husband or wife.

The word of God tells us to flee fornication. It also tells us as believers not to be unequally yoked with unbelievers. If the gentleman in question had really loved her, even if he was unsaved, he would have married her and given her his name and not left her to bring up their four children all by herself. Sometimes one may find one self in an unexpected position and may slip, but the secret is not to stay in that position, but to pick yourself up, dust yourself off and continue running on for the Lord. This is what she did. God forgives. But there are always consequences for sin.

If one cannot contain oneself when single, then that particular individual is not ready for marriage and is in need of some serious spiritual and psychological help. This can culminate in a very explosive situation, because when married and marital problems present themselves, their respective partner may not be able to fulfill their many needs. Eventually adultery will take place resulting eventually in divorce.

If you need a husband or wife do not be too bashful to tell God all your desires, because he knows anyway, so you cannot fool Him. Tell Him what you want. We should all pray for the partners that God has in store for us. Even parents need to pray that God would send the right person into their children's lives to be their life partner. This is very important for a successful godly marriage.

WHO SHOULD MARRY

"And the Lord God said, it is not good that the man should be alone; I will make an help meet for him." Genesis 2:18 (KJV).

It is the view of many that God created Eve because Adam was all alone and lonely. This was indeed not the case. He was alone but he certainly was not lonely, because he did not even realize that he was lonely, however God saw it fit to give him a companion. The animals in the Garden of Eden all had their companions so why not man, this also led to the propagation of the human race. One's mind should not be so focused on having a mate that everything else becomes dim in comparison.

A person need to become occupied in the things of God, because when this is done then, He will in turn grant us the very desires of our heart. God realized that Adam needed help, so he created Eve, however, it is important for one to realize and understand exactly what kind of "help" she was created to provide.

When most of us think of choosing a mate it is usually with the attitude of trying to eliminate the problem of being alone. However, being alone is a problem that can only be resolved by having a personal relationship with our Lord and Savior, Jesus Christ. The purpose of having a mate is to provide the help that one needs in one's relationship with God. At this point many people may start to have serious objections to this statement, but just have patience and let me explain.

Not everyone needs a mate to help him or her in his or her respective relationship with God. Both Paul and Jesus made reference to this fact. Paul made reference to it in First Corinthians, chapter seven, as a "gift". In **Matthew 19:12** Jesus states,

"For there are some eunuchs, which are born from their mother's womb: and there are some eunuchs, which were made eunuchs of men: and there be eunuchs, which have made themselves eunuchs for the kingdom of heaven's sake. He that is able to receive it, let him receive it." **(KJV)**

In the preceding passage, we see three divisions by Jesus. The first being that there are some people who have absolutely no sexual desire because they were born that way. This may be because of something physical, or it may be psychological. However, one thing is certain- **they have no desire for any kind of sexual involvement or relationship with another person.** In this day and age, I believe that this kind of person is very hard to find.

The second being categorized as a group that was made that way by men, **they are physically incapable of having sexual intercourse** becoming eunuchs by force. This second grouping is hardly seen today also. In times gone by when a kingdom attacked and conquered another nation, they killed or castrated the sons of the king and those of royalty, thus making sure that they cannot have any sons or daughters that can claim their rightful position as heir to their respective thrones. They were also forced into the roles of servants to wait on their new masters. However, this kind of punishment today would be considered atrocities against the rights of a human being.

The third and last group are those who make themselves eunuchs for the sake of the Gospel. **Those persons who of their own free will decide to stay single and deny themselves the benefit of having a wife or a husband and devote themselves to living a very celibate life.** However it is God who endows a person with that grace, and it is indeed a grace. Paul received that grace from God hence he was able to stay single and be all that God wanted him to be.

There is a clear distinction between that third group and the first two. The first two are incapable of sexual relationship, because there is some element in their lives that makes them incapable of forming that kind of relationship. However, with the third group, it is not because of something mental or psychological, but it is a quality decision that an individual makes within his or her heart. They put away all the desires that they may have had of engaging in any kind of physical and sexual relationship with a mate, and giving themselves fully and solely to the work of the Lord. The ability to do this is referred to as a "gift". Nuns and priests usually do this. A good example of this is Mother Theresa who forsake all, wealth, family and position to follow Christ. Whatever we do or give up for Christ we can be assured that we have our reward and crowns to receive on judgment day.

To state quite plainly, if one experiences any form of sexual desire, and this sexual desire can be aroused within them, then one is definitely not a eunuch and would indeed need a mate. If the "gift" that Paul spoke of in First Corinthians, chapter seven is not manifested is one's life then one will need help in their relationship with God and this is where a mate comes in.

Paul states clearly in First Corinthians 7:2 *"To avoid fornication, let every man have his own wife, and let every woman have her own husband."* (KJV) Any man or woman who cannot otherwise avoid fornication should have a mate – even those who have previously married and are now single; whether by divorce or by their spouse's death.

In Paul statement in **1 Corinthians 7:7-9** explains:

> *"I would prefer that all of you were as I am; but each one has a special gift from God, one person this gift, another one that gift".*
> *vr.7 (KJV)*

There are two words in the Greek text that should be looked at and explained to achieve the full extent and meaning that Paul wanted to extend. The first is "all", in the phrase *"I would prefer that all of you were as I am"*. The Greek word is *pantas*, the plural of *pas*.' In the KJV it states, *"I would that all men were even I myself."* At one glance, one may think that it refers to all humanity, however it does not, it deals with individuals.

The New Living Translation (NLT) has a more realistic translation and refers to the individuals within the totality of humanity. There is no person that Paul refers to that God cannot enable to be like him, if it is God's will. If God's grace was sufficient to enable Paul to be single and accomplish what He wanted him to accomplish, then it would and should be sufficient for any one individual to do likewise by the grace of God.

Hence, if God allows His child to take this path in his or her life, He will also give them the necessary grace and enablement. God will never lead us where the grace of God is inadequate to keep us. To put it plainly, Paul is not saying that he wants all people to accomplish what he did by being single as he was, but that anyone can abide holy within the single life no matter how long the time frame may be. It is God that leads him or her in that path in life. If God leads a person, then He will most definitely give him or her the grace and enablement to be victorious over his or her sexual desires.

> **1 Corinthians 7:8-9**
> *"Now, to the unmarried and to the widows I say that it would be better for you to continue to live alone as I do vr.8*
> *But if you cannot restrain yours desires, go ahead and marry it is better to marry than to burn with passion." vr.9* (NLT)

This scripture should not be taken out of context by persons to fulfill their own personal needs and desires. There must be a proper balance of the Word of God. The Scriptures states that if we cannot contain ourselves we should marry and it is in marrying that a husband and wife help each other out, thus keeping their sexual desires under control. It is because of marriage that each is able to go before God with a pure heart because He has sanctioned and blessed their sexual union.

However, persons who have serious sexual problems and cannot contain themselves should not use marriage as a "copout" or "porn". If they enter a marriage not being able to contain themselves, then problems will definitely arise in that marriage, because infidelity will occur and it will just be a matter of time before the marriage breaks down if help is not sort.

If we as human beings cannot contain and control our sexual desires then we are no better than the other animals, which do what they want when they want. However, even animals have their own code of conduct. God has implanted into man (man and woman) the ability of freedom of choice. We as human beings can either choose to go God's way, which is a life that is pleasing to Him and in obedience to His Words; or the way of the flesh, which is the way of the devil, or live in disobedience. The Scriptures states that we are to flee unrighteousness and choose life. Righteous is obedience unto the spirit of the living God.

CHOOSING THE RIGHT PARTNER

In **Genesis 2:22**

> *"And the rib, which the Lord God hath taken from man, made he a woman, <u>and brought her unto the man.</u>" <u>(KJV)</u>*

This scripture states the true pattern of God, the presenting of the woman to the man. A person may pray for a husband or wife, but then have to wait upon God to present him or her. If one does otherwise he can find himself operating in God's permissive will and not His perfect will.

When God brought Eve to Adam, he did not have to accept her, he could have told God that he did not want or need her. However, he accepted his father's choice of mate for him, and was very pleased with him wife, for he said in **Gen. 2:23**

> *"At last!"she is part of my flesh and bone She will be called 'woman' because she was taken out of man" (NLT)*

Every day that a person lives there are choices that must be made and they can either be good or bad. One has to decide with a little leading from the Lord, to allow him to do what is right and pleasing in His sight.

Sometimes God could present a man to a woman or a woman to a man, but he or she may have dreams about what their "dream person" should look like. If it is a male he may visualize what work he must be doing and what car he must be driving - or if it is a female - what kind of figure and color of hair she must have. However not checking on his or her spiritual life may totally disregard the person that God has presented to them. God knows the path in life that He has for every single person. God knows the beginning from the end, and we don't know our future, but He does. He wrote the book and He knows the final chapter.

One should never allow their relationship with God to slip in order to have a mate. God is a jealous God and any person or thing that is placed before Him, He will remove in order to save our soul. Before a person thinks about dating he needs to spend time and work on his personal, intimate eternal relationship with God. Only when he is secure in that relationship, will there be a successful personal, intimate, until-death-do-us-part relationship with another human being.

However as believers, one should not make a decision to get married lightly. Time, effort and much thought should be given into making this decision, with the ultimate part being seeking the face of God in order to make the right decision, and having God's blessing on the union.

SEXUAL SIN?

In today's society, because of sin, there has been a creeping decrease in the moral standards in the society. What was once considered right and pleasing to God and His Word, is now considered wrong and man is now doing whatsoever is right in his own eyes. The Bible states in Corinthians 6 that those who indulge in sexual sin **i.e.** (those not showing a repentant attitude by a changed way of life), *will* have no share or place in the Kingdom of Heaven. Those included are fornicators, adulterers, male and female prostitutes, homosexuals, lesbians and others who indulge in sin. Make no doubt about it, sin will be judged.
    Sexual sin always ends in destruction, and operates like a thief in the night, creeping upon you, and before you know it you are caught. Proverbs mentions a great deal about this sin, **(Proverbs 7:6-7, 9-11, 13, 15, 21-23)** Solomon again warns young men by his observation: -

> *I was looking out the window of my house one day. vr.6*
> *and saw a simple minded young man who lacked common sense. vr.7*
> *He was crossing the street near the*

house of an immoral woman He was strolling down the path by her house. vr.9

at twilight, as the day was fading, as the dark of night set in. vr.10

The woman approached him, dressed seductively and sly at heart. vr.11

She threw her arms around him and kissed him, and with a brazen look she said..vr.13

It 's you I was looking for! I came out to find you, and here you are vr.15

So she seduced him with her pretty speech. With her flattery she enticed him vr.21

He followed her at once, like an ox going to the slaughter or like a trapped stag, vr.22

Awaiting the arrow that would pierce its heart. He was like a bird fling into a snare, little knowing it would cost him his life. vr.23

Don't let your hearts stray away towards her. Don't wonder down Her wayward path. vr.25

For she has been the ruin of many; numerous men have been her victims vr.26

Her house is the road to the grave. Her bedroom is s the den of death. vr.27 (NLT)

In **Prov.6:** Solomon admonishes young men: -

My son, obey your father's commands, and don't neglect your mother's teaching. **vr.22**

The correction of discipline is the way of life. **vr.23**

> *These commands and this teaching will keep you from the immoral woman, from the smooth tongue of an adulterous woman.* **vr.24**
> *Don't lust for her beauty. Don't let her coyness seduce you.* **vr.25**
> *For a prostitute will bring you to poverty, and sleeping with another man's wife may cost you your very life.* **vr.26**
> *Can a man scoop fire into his lap and not be burned?* **vr.27**
> *Can he walk on hot coals and not blister his feet?"* **vr.28 (NLT)**

Regard lust as a warning sign of danger ahead. When you notice that you are being attracted to and enticed by a person of the opposite sex or preoccupied with thoughts of him or her, your desires may lead you to sin. Ask God to help you change your desires before you are snared.

Solomon continues to state in Proverbs 9, how women will try to entice a man by telling him:

> *"Stolen water is refreshing; food eaten in secret tastes the best!* **vr.9:17**
> *But the men don't realize that her former guests are now in the grave.* **vr.18 (NLT)**

There is something hypnotic and touching about wickedness. One sin leads to another; sinful behavior may seem more exciting than the Christian life. However, don't be deceived, sin is dangerous. Some people may argue that it is all right to break God's law in relation to sexual sin if nobody gets hurt. However contrary to this belief somebody always gets hurt. It hurts God because it shows that we prefer following our own desires instead of the leading of the Holy Spirit. It hurt others because it violates the commitment so necessary to a relationship.

Sexual temptations are difficult to withstand because they appeal to the normal and natural desires that God has given us. Before engaging in any illicit sexual act, a long look should be taken at those who have participated in it and observe the outcome. It deeply affects a person's personality, their physical body and also their spiritual life. When we become Christians, the Holy Spirit comes and lives in us. When we sin in our bodies we disrespect and embarrass the Holy Spirit that dwells within us. If we continue to sin, the Holy Spirit will depart for God is sinless and cannot be a part of sin.

1 Corinthians 6:13-20

...But our bodies were not made for sexual immorality. They were made for the Lord, and the Lord cares about our bodies. **vr.13**

Should a man take his body, which belongs to Christ, and join it to a prostitute? Never! **vr.15**

And don't you know that if a man joins himself to a prostitute, he becomes one body with her? For the Scriptures states, "Two are united into one" **vr.16**

But the person who is joined to the Lord becomes one spirit with him." **vr.17**

Run away from sexual sin! No other sin so clearly affects the body as this one does. For sexual immorality is a sin against your own body. **vr.18**

Or don't you know that your body is the

> *temple of the Holy Spirit, who lives in you and was given to you by God? You do not belong to yourself.* **vr.19.**
> *For God brought you with a high price. So you must honor God with your body.* **vr.20.** *(NLT)*

Christians are free to be all they can be for God, but they are not free from God.

> **Rom.1:24-28**
> *So God let them go ahead and do whatsoever shameful things their hearts desired. As a result, they did vile and degrading things with each other's bodies.* **vr.24**
> *In stead of believing what they knew was the truth about God, they deliberately choose to believe lies.* **vr.25**
> *That is why God abandoned them to their shameful desires. Even the women turned against the natural way to have sex and instead indulged in sex with each other.* **v.26**
> *And the men, instead of having normal sexual relationship with women, burned with lust for each other. Men did shameful things with other men and as a result, suffered within themselves. The penalty they so richly deserved.* **vr.27** *(NLT)*

For a man's ways are in full view of the Lord, and He examines all his paths. Sexual pleasure or sexual fulfillment is part of God's purpose for sex in marriage and such experience is designed for the commitment and trust of marriage. Outside of marriage sex ultimately leads to guilt, loss of self-respect and away from the will of God.

Social promiscuity and an alternative lifestyle seem to be accepted as the norm in today's society and keeping one's virginity and sexual abstinence are considered by the world to be abnormal.

The breakdown in moral values happens in every strata of society. Thus children are brought into the world not having the benefit of having two loving parents to bring them up and teach them in the way that they should go, implanting into them moral and spiritual values.

These situations happen particularly in depressed neighborhoods where crime and sex go hand in hand. In the middle and upper levels of society, promiscuity also exists but not in the same dimension. Sex is just as prominent but because of education and the availability of finance and choices, the consequences do not seem as alarming.

When a young person engages in illicit sex, the last thing that she usually has on her mind is pregnancy or getting infected with HIV (Human Immunodeficiency Virus).

However with the emergence of HIV everybody is on the same level or playing field, because Aids does not respect age and crosses all races, socioeconomic barriers and every and anyone one can get it. All it takes is to have unprotected sex once, in order to contract the HIV virus. This virus in turn leads to Aids and in the end, causes death. This has been the fate of millions of people who have succumbed to the HIV virus, throughout the world. The West Indies is no exception. The number of persons affected by HIV is increasing rapidly.

The world has now become a global village and every single country is affected by HIV in some way or another, be it **economic** - because of loss of income and the enormous cost of medicine for those affected by it; **physical** – millions of people have died all over the world; **social** – because of the number of families that have been affected by the untimely death of their loved ones. Most of the population who have died and are infected are the young. Families now have to go on, some of them without their mother or father or both parents. In some cases, while often parents survive their child or children. I believe that every couple, who decides to get married today, even though they are Christians, should have a blood test done before they get married.

The church is a spiritual hospital and there would be persons joining the various assemblies who are HIV positive. This is not intended to alienate the person with the virus, but to protect the innocent. If the person with the virus decides to marry, then both parties ought to be aware of the consequences and decide how far they will allow the relationship to proceed thus making informed decisions. As I stated before, this is not to be bias, but it is necessary in order to protect the innocent parties in question.

Sex is one of the most important and effective tools that the enemy uses; hence one must at all times be vigilant, especially as single persons not to be caught in this web. An example of this illicit act is Monica L. and President Clinton. Both of them paid a very high price and her name is known all over the world for engaging in an illicit sexual affair with the then president who was very much married at the time, and still continues to remain married to his wife.

I have heard my mother say from the time I was a child, that it is very bad practice for a single person - especially a young single woman - to become sexually involved, and "have and affair" with a married man. She said that it "blighted" the person for the rest of her life. The vows states – 'What the Lord has joined together, let no man put asunder.' It is when a third party enters a marriage that turmoil begins in a marriage. This was not meant to be.

It is only now that I am an adult and matured in Christ that I can fully understand the full extent of exactly what she meant and the spiritual implications and consequences that may arise when one enters into this kind of illicit relationship.

The Word of God has always had the solution and the world is now trying to adopt it as a last resort. The condom, which have been endorsed in the past and are still being endorsed and are passing out even to school children, has failed. The only way to prevent HIV - outside of not being infected by tainted blood - is by abstinence. It comes right back to what God says in the Word of God.

2 Timothy 2:22 tells us to: -

"flee also youthful lusts: but follow righteousness, charity, peace, with them that call on the Lord out of a pure heart." **KJV**

I also know a few "Christian young ladies" who have had abortions. They had the abortions because they felt that they did not want to go through the embarrassment and public humiliation of having a child out of wedlock and be a reproach to the church. However, they continually have emotional problems in relation to their choice when they realized what they did. They compounded their sin of illicit sex, by adding murder to it.

Any young Christian woman who engages in pre-marital sexual activity and gets pregnant and has the baby, I applaud her (not for the illicit affairs) but for going through with the pregnancy. It is a very strong person, who is sincerely repentant, and does that in light of the embarrassment and all the other consequences that go along with it. The fornication is the sin, not the child. A child is a gift from the Lord. However, because of how it was conceived there will most definitely be certain repercussions that she will have to face every day of her life. There are always consequences for sin.

The Apostle Paul also admonishes believers in 1 Cor. 10: 12-13.

> *"If you think you are standing strong, be careful, for you, too, may fall into the same sin."* Vr.12
> *But remember that the temptations that come into our life are no different from what others experience. And God is faithful. He will keep the temptation from becoming so strong that you can't stand up against it. When you are tempted, he will show you a way out so that you will not give in to it."* vr.13 (NLT)

If you think you cannot succeed in a commitment to premarital purity, you are not too weak; you may just not be relying on God enough. Philippians 4:13 states that *"I can do everything through him who gives me strength"* Just remember that we can do all things through Christ, and he is no respecter of persons. Everyone is God's favorite. You are God's favorite. You can do it.

SEX BEFORE MARRIAGE

Sex before marriage is called premarital sex. The command of our God is of course sufficient reason to refrain from premarital sex. Premarital sex always leaves scars and these scars have an effect on you even years after. In the moment of passion, the persons involved do not think of the implications and consequences that could occur because of the heightened emotions. However, one cannot violate the command of God concerning something so wonderful, and not be hurt.

The young woman who violates God's commands concerning sex feels used and cheated. She realizes too late, that she has "lost" a most precious possession, her virginity.

The young man also loses something when he goes too far before marriage, giving it away cheaply. The loss of innocence, through sexual impurity, is as real for a boy/male as it is for the girl/female. He may deceive himself into believing that gratification of the moment will make that loss worthwhile. But he too will find, to his grief, that it does not. God will not be mocked.

Some claim the "right" to premarital sex because they are engaged. They believe that their expressions of commitment to each other make it right for them to violate God's will, and God's law. Being engaged is not a right for the parties involved to become sexually intimate. Engagement is a promise to marry, not a marriage. Young ladies, Young men, you have come too far, you can wait a little longer. It is God's will that sexual activities be engaged in, only in marriage. It is only God who unites two persons in marriage, using the church and the state to be His means to unite them.

There are certain risks that go along with engaging in premarital sex. Some of these are: -

- Contracting STDs, particularly Aids, which leads to death.
- Infertility from STD's.
- The transference of demonic spirits from one party to the next.
- Damaged or lost relationships because of sexual involvement.
- Depression because of the non-commitment of the other party.
- Insecurity.
- Distrust.
- Damaging future marriage, because of a coloured past.
- Sexual dysfunction, because of pornography, masturbation and sex.

- The risk of pregnancy. Only abstinence is totally safe.
- Damaging your testimony as a Christian engaging in premarital sex.
- You pledge allegiance to another lord.
- You grieve the Holy Spirit.
- Disobeying the will of God contained in the Bible.

True love always waits. As a Christian you must not let anyone say to you that your love must be proven by sexual favours. True love will not want to have sex with a person and cause them heartache and pain. If you are pressured to have sex, then you are not loved, but rather you are being used. He does not care about you, and you should let him know your beliefs and the stand that you have taken. If he breaks up with you because of this, then you are better off without him anyway. A person, and in particular a young person should know that they are fearfully and wonderfully made and no one should let their past dictate their future, for when God made us he made us with destiny in mind for us.

STIMULATING ONE'S SELF (MASTURBATION)

This is a subject that is considered taboo in the Church of Jesus Christ and is not broached or touched on at all because of its delicate nature. I did not want to put the heading as simply "Masturbation", hence the inclusion of the title "Stimulating One's Self – Masturbation." This expansion of the topic may give one a broader concept of the subject.

I have been pondering this subject for quite a while, however, it was not a topic that I intended to include in this book. I was forced to change my mind and write about it when I realized, to my dismay, that this is a secret that the church hardly speaks about, but is a practice that many Christians engage in.

In my quest to deal with my own sexual feelings I asked a few persons how they dealt with their sexual desires when they arose, and the more I asked the older single people, the more the subject of masturbation came up. As one of my friends said to me " Barbara don't you know that this is what most of the single people in the church do?" I was taken aback at her answer. I knew that single people in the world did it, but I did not bargain for the extent to which the Christian community engaged in it.

The people in the world and that include Christians as well, go as far as using what they call "adult toys" to help them achieve sexual satisfaction. However, the Christian, the church folks, they should know better and not be led to follow the trend in today's immoral society.

My friend continued to tell me that people do not speak about it, however, most single people in the church engage in it. I was very much surprised, hence the relevance of this topic. I just cannot see an anointed man or woman of God functioning heavily under the anointing of the Holy Spirit, engaging in this practice.

The Bible states in Romans 12:1-4

> *"I beseech you brethren, by the mercies of God, that you present your bodies a living sacrifice, holy, acceptable unto God, which is your reasonable service. And be not conformed to this world, but be ye transformed by the renewing of your mind, that ye may prove what is that good, and acceptable, and perfect will of God." (KJV)*

Spiritual warfare should not be taken lightly. We are in a war, thus one should behave, as a good soldier of Jesus

Christ, braving the storms and the fiery darts of the enemy **that will**, (**not might**), come our way. One needs to be girded at all times and be fully armed for the onslaught of the enemy. How can a person say that he or she is fully armed for spiritual warfare and engage in masturbation? This definitely ought not to happen. That person would not be able to come up against and take authority over the spirit of lust and be victorious, because his or her armor would be down for one, and also they would have no authority over that spirit, because he or she had succumbed to it.

When a person engages in masturbation, at the time of climax, they are not in control of their emotions and thought, and an entrance is left wide open for unclean and demonic spirits to enter into them. The blood of Jesus does not cover them, because they are engaging in sin, and their spiritual defenses are down. Also when a person is masturbating, they usually will visualize a person or persons when committing the act.

This alone is sin, on top of that, they may conjure up some form of fantasy person, again opening the doorway for demonic spirits to participate in this act with them.

A person can only have authority and be victorious over demonic spirits when they are overcomers. We are all supposed to be victors in Christ Jesus.

SINGLE PERSONS CO-HABITING TOGETHER (COMMON LAW MARRIAGE)

A common law marriage occurs when two persons, usually a male and a female cohabit (as husband and wife), outside the bounds of holy matrimony.

This is a situation that a "Born Again" Christian person

should avoid. It is unholy, and is against the Word of God. No matter how one dresses it up, it is sin. What is even worse are two persons who are still legally married to their respective spouses and have children from those unions, cohabiting with someone other than their legal spouse as husband and wife. God cannot bless that relationship. This relationship is doomed from the start and unknown to them, they are being set up by Satan, the great deceiver for pain, disappointment and heartache. Single persons should never find themselves in this situation; more so, single believers.

I have had to counsel with a very pretty young woman some time ago. In talking to her she told me that she had a child who was about one and a half years old, and she was still living at home with her mother. As I continued talking to her, I found out that her boyfriend, the child's father, was also living with her at home. I then asked her if he supported her and the baby, and to my surprise she told me no, because both of them were not working. Her mother supported her financially. I, in turn, told her that he could not truly love her because they were living together and she had his child, but he did not see it fit to honor her in marriage and supply her financial needs. He certainly was not worth losing her salvation over.

Any young, self-respecting woman should never settle for this kind of relationship. If a man tells you, as a young single person, that he loves you and wants to move in with you or you with him, let him prove that he really loves you by marrying you and giving you his name, then he can have all of you. It is the only way that God would sanction and bless that relationship.

A woman should never be so afraid of losing the man in her life, that she has to prove her love to him by sleeping, or moving in with him. If he really loves her and is sensitive to her feelings and the consequences and responsibilities that would occur because of this act, he would not do it, especially if she is a virgin. It is better to lose him than to lose the love of God. I have found out that, as a single woman, that I can have a husband who will never leave me nor forsake me, and his name is Jesus.

A woman should never have to 'buy' a man in order for him to stay with her. Some women 'buy' the men with whom they say they are in love with. They buy them brand name clothes, cell phones, cars and even houses and support them financially, just because they do not want to lose them. These things may keep them for a while, but they would not stick around for very long, because who knows they may even find others who may be able to provide for them better.

Also, the very nature that God created in the male, would start to rebel and after a while, because his maleness is being threatened, and he will not feel comfortable in that kind of relationship. Men were created with attributes of being providers and not receivers. This kind of relationship goes against God's plan for the male (man). They were meant to be the head and in charge of their respective households, responsible for their families with the woman being their helpmate.

Also, a Christian woman should be a virtuous woman as described in Proverbs 31 by one of the wisest persons who ever lived, King Solomon. He emphasized how she should conduct herself in a godly manner. In fact any Christian man should be proud to ask her out, that is if she is single. I have been a Christian for a very long time, and I have seen Christian women throw themselves at single Christian men and sometimes even married men in the church. Sometimes the ladies because of their behavior make some of the men who join the church 'run out' or leave the church.

I have also seen and witnessed many times how Christian women compete among themselves when a single male join their assembly. They may even compromise their positions as Christians, just to be the one who catches his eye. This however reflects negatively on Christian women. New converts are very impressionable and are familiar with the mode of conduct of women in the world. Hence when they come into the church they expect and should see godly Christian women.

Women need not settle for any man who comes along, because they feel that they are getting old. A real Christian man would not be attracted to any woman who displays loose moral standards, and who would jump into bed with him if she was asked. He will hardly ever marry her because of her lack of moral standards.

A man loves a challenge women, and a woman who would stand up for what is right in God's sight with out fear or favor, he will appreciate and admire. If he does not then he is not worth the trouble. Men, a woman is just the same, she would love a man who loves God and would put God first. A man who could be the prophet and priest of his home and who would love her and be faithful to her. I do not think that that is too much to ask.

When a man is looking for a wife, along with the woman's appearance he would not want to marry a person that he cannot respect and be proud of. My philosophy is as I tell the young ladies "no ring no thing". It is not worth it, defiling your self and denying and embarrassing the Spirit of God that dwells in you. It is worth it to wait because God honors sex and it is sacred in his sight. If God can do the impossible for Abraham and Sarah and give them a baby when she was past childbearing age, He can do the same for you too. For with God all things are possible, you just have to believe God for your miracle.

No self-respecting young woman should take it upon herself to voluntarily go and live with a man even if he is supporting her; this goes for the man to. This is what my pastor calls being a one-man prostitute. You have to cook for him, wash his clothes, see about his children – because if you are living together then you may ultimately have children - and take care of all his other needs, which at times can be very demanding, and may not even get paid for doing them.

I would advise any young person, woman or man who has entered into a common law relationship to come out of it because it not pleasing to the Lord Jesus Christ. He came and died for our sins and that we might have life and have it more abundantly, because of His great love for us. No matter what problem a person may have gone and is going through, God can solve it because He is the great problem solver.

When Moses and the Israelites were at the Red Sea with no way out and the Egyptians were coming behind them to kill them, it seemed like a hopeless situation, but God. God came through for Moses and the Israelite people and made a way where there seemed to be none. He can make a way in the desert and a highway in the wilderness, for there is nothing too hard for our God to do. He did it for me and He can do it for anyone who will call upon Him for help. For His Word says that a broken and contrite heart He will not despise.

One may say Doctor Barbara, "you do not know what I am going through, I have children for this man, I am not gainfully employed and I live at him". Well take consolation that you are not the first person to find yourself in this predicament, nor will you be the last. To give you some very practical examples of a number of women who were in your position.

A couple of women over a period of time visited our church and after some time they gave their lives to the Lord Jesus Christ. However, they each had a problem, they were living in common law relationships. After my pastor spoke to them about it and counseled with them, all except one eventually got married to the men with whom they were living with. The men loved them enough to give up their bachelorhood, giving them their names and in so doing, gave them back their self-respect as women with worth. The one, who did not want to get married, she decided that the pastor was too harsh and left the church, is now single. The man with whom she was living with left her for someone else.

God did not promise us a life without trials, but if we know for a surety that He holds our hands, then we need not worry. He will not allow us to go through anything where His grace cannot keep us. He is able to do for us, more than we could possibly ask for or think.

Some of these men whom the ladies married, are now saved and are serving the Lord. The others, though they have not fully committed themselves to Christ, have gained a great fear and respect for God and it is just a matter of time before they too come into the fold of Jesus Christ. Jesus is no respecter of persons. What He has done for these women He could do for you. He can make a highway in the desert and He is our way maker. There is nothing too hard for God to do, and **He can do anything but fail**. What a God we have, and He is on our side.

AN ALTERNATIVE LIFE STYLE

The term "An alternative life style" is an expression that has come into vogue in recent times. It is used in the case of same sex relationships to the stage where co-habiting, even legally, is the norm. These are men and women who have left the natural use of their bodies and have done that which the Bible calls unseemly.

To affirm homosexuality is to deny God's creative power. Homosexual conduct is a sin. It is against nature and against God's creative design. Men are now marrying men and women and now marrying women and cohabiting, and the society finds nothing wrong with that. Promiscuity only leads to the breakdown of the family structure and the society at large. This relationship is abnormal in the sight of God, because God created 'man and woman' to be together, not man and man or woman and woman.

In Leviticus 18:22-23 God commands His people "*Do not practice homosexuality; it is a detestable sin.*" (NLT). It is the sexual act between two people of the same gender. Young men and women do not be encouraged into this life style, because it will only lead you down the path of death. It is easy to get into but is a very difficult lifestyle to get out of and it is the reason for God's destruction of Sodom and Gomorrah by God.(Gen.19: 1-29).

The Word of God states in Leviticus 20:13

> *"The penalty for homosexual acts is death to both parties. They have committed a detestable act and are guilty of a capital offence." (NLT).*

If anyone feels that those laws were only for Old Testaments times, the New Testament also condemns homosexuality.

In 1 Corinthians 6: 9 Paul admonishes believers that

> *" those who do wrong will have no share in the Kingdom of God. Don't fool yourselves. Those who indulge in sexual sin, who are idol worshippers, adulterers, male prostitutes, homosexuals .... None of these will have a share in the Kingdom of God."*(NLT)

Paul writes in **Romans 1:24-28**

> *So God let them go ahead into every sort of sex sin, and do whatever they wanted to- yes, vile and sinful things with each other's*

bodies. vr.24

Instead of believing what was the truth about God, They deliberately chose to believe lies. vr.25

That is why God let go of them and let them do all these evil things, so that even their women turned against God's natural plan for them and indulged in sex with each other. vr.26.

And the men, instead of having normal sex relationship with women, burned with lust for each other, men doing shameful things with other men and, as a result, getting paid within their our souls with the penalty they so richly deserved."vr.27

When they refused to acknowledge God, he abandoned them to their evil minds and let them do things that should never be done.vr.28 (NIV)

Man has left God out of their homes, schools, institutions and invariable out of their lives, thus leaving and paving the way for anything that is not of God to enter and have complete control. As Christians and as children of God we have the power through Christ Jesus to stand up and declare righteousness and holiness in the land (irrespective of who may feel offended.)

DEALING WITH ONE'S SEXUALITY

I have now found myself single and have had to make the necessary adjustments in my life. Making this adjustment has not been an easy feat for me, and seeing that it was not easy for me I decided to find out from some of my single friends, what they did when their natural sexual urges occurred.

I have realized since I am once more single, that not enough time and effort have been given to understanding the many challenges that a single person goes through everyday. Most married people are usually so taken up in their daily lives, that once married, it seems that they forget the trials that a single person goes through on a daily basis. I know I did, until I became single again.

I realized that I had some serious sexual problems and had to find answers to deal with my emotions in relation to my own sexuality. I had been married for about ten years and was accustomed to having marital relations, which are normal for married people. It was hard and a struggle at first, because I suddenly found myself single and emotionally traumatized. I was accustomed to it and my body was accustomed to it. Now what does a person do about it? The answer for this can be found in the chapter "**The Answer**", later in this book.

The only time that a previously married person or someone who has been sexually active and who is now single would have negative feelings in relation to the sexual act, is if she has had a very bad experience in that area, and probably if she experienced a very nasty divorce. Even if a person decides that she does not want to have a relationship with another man after having been divorced or separated from her spouse, or her husband may have died, she will still experience normal sexual feelings, because it is part of human nature.

When a person is experiencing a very stressful situation, like divorce, and it prolongs for an extended period of time, the effects of this can be seen manifesting in their bodies in various forms of diseases.

Sigmund Freud the well-known theorist of the psychosexual developmental stages of man theorized and believed that man's sexual instinct is the most important factor influencing personality and the relationship between mind and pleasure. This he postulated is present at birth and then develops through a series of psychosexual stages namely the oral, anal, phallic, latent and genital stages.

Sexuality, in Freudian usage, is not restricted to sexual intercourse but rather, each stage concerns a particular erogenous zone, which is a part of the body that provides pleasurable sensations and around which conflict arises. If the conflict is not resolved, then the child may develop a fixation. A fixation can be described as an arrested development at a psychosexual stage, occurring because of excess gratification or frustration at that particular stage. One of the fixations which takes place at the Phallic stage which is from ages 3 – 6 years is masturbation. At this age he postulated that boys play with their penis, and if there is a fixation at this stage, then it continues well into their adult years.

Sex And The Single Person

I was curious to hear how individuals dealt with their feelings when they were sexually aroused particularly because holiness, fornication and abstinence are preached in churches. But telling the single men and women how to deal with these real and natural desires are not freely discussed at all. They are in fact "taboo". The Church of Jesus Christ needs to get real and address these crucial areas because it affects a large number of the Christian population.

One of the persons that I asked was a Christian young lady about fifteen or sixteen years old. Her answer to my question about what a young person like herself would do when these feelings occurred was to sublimate - get busy doing something. I asked her this important question because in my eyes she looked like a very responsible and mature person for her age. Nevertheless she looked a bit apprehensive before answering the question. That was probably because she was shocked and a little taken aback by my question, that being the last question in her mind that she thought I would ask her. However, that was part of the answer that I was looking for.

I then asked a single woman about forty years old who had accepted the Lord about thirteen years, to tell me what she does when she gets these desires. She also was a bit shocked at my question, and thought that I wanted to "mind her business", but I explained to her that I was very serious and really wanted her to give me an honest answer.

To my surprise she was very glad to have somebody to 'vent' her pent-up rage and anger against. She told me that when these desires occur she cries out to the Lord to take the feelings away from her and sometimes she goes to bed and falls asleep and it disappears, otherwise she paces the floor. She next started to complain to me about the Lord.

She told me that she could not take it any longer because she has been waiting for the Lord to send her a husband for years and she still did not have one and she had wasted all her youth. She had a child and was in a common law relationship when she got saved, so she had experienced intimate relations. She knew about sexual intercourse. She made me to understand that it was something that she had enjoyed.

She continued to tell me that she had been faithful to the Lord, so how come He did not give her a husband? In between the conversation she mentioned the common law husband that she had before she got saved and how he was the only man that she had ever really loved and that she had enjoyed quite an exciting sex life with him.

She said that the gentleman in question still loved her but she did not want to continue their relationship when she got saved. I, in turn, had to counsel and tell her that the reason that the Lord could not give her a husband was because she had kept the past boyfriend so close to her heart and mind, that the Lord could not give her one, there was no room for the new husband to occupy.

I continued to tell her that because they were sexually involved, that there was a 'soul tie' or bond between them that needed to be broken, and she had to be the one to break it, because he is still unsaved. He in turn had moved on with his life, because he is at present in a common law relationship with another woman, and there are children from that union.

The breaking of the "soul tie" could be done by her renouncing and breaking all ties between them in the spiritual realm; leaving room for God to freely bring a husband into her life. All this time she was the one blocking God from giving her the husband that she so desperately wanted. This is one of the reasons why a person should not engage in premarital sex, there are repercussions in the natural as well as in the spiritual realm.

I also spoke to a Christian gentleman asking him the same question and his reply to my question was to ask God to take it away, and if he does not, then you could always masturbate, I was very taken aback by that answer. I was taken aback because he was a minister and very active in church ministry. He even confessed to me that he had an affair with one of the choir leaders in the church, and had to leave the particular church that he was attending at the time and joined another church just to get out of that relationship.

I spoke to yet another gentleman and asked him what he did when these desires arose. He told me very seriously that before he got saved he was actually in a common law relationship with someone, and when he got saved he terminated the relationship.

He continued to tell me that a little while after that he had been coerced into having an affair with a particular young lady that he was attracted to, although she was not saved. At the point when he was about to give in to this young lady's charms, his pastor called him and prophetically told him "do not mar your testimony". He told me that from that time until when I spoke to him, that any time situations come up whereby he could be tempted, he remembers and heeds the words of his pastor. At present he is married to a woman that he adores and is enjoying married life.

If a person waits on God, He would grant that person the very desires of his or her heart. God knows the beginning from the end and know what will be good or bad for us. We just have to keep on trusting Him and know for a surety that what the devil means for bad, God has a way of turning it around for His Good. The person that we are at present is, determined by all the experiences that the Lord permitted us to go through. Satan cannot touch us without God's permission; therefore we are much richer and better equipped for life because of all the experiences that we have been through. Also, our place of pain becomes our place of gain.

SEXUAL INSTINCT

Man's sexual drive is an instinctive, God given part of his human nature, which is meant however, to be controlled by man himself. The word "man" is used here in the genetic sense as referring to both man and woman and the same rules apply to both. A man is not permitted to enjoy a greater liberty in the expression of his sexual instinct just because it may be stronger than the woman.

God said in Genesis, let us (the Holy Trinity) make man, in our image and likeness. When Adam sinned and disobeyed God, God's spirit departed from him. God used to come down and talk to Adam in the cool of the day, face to face. After he sinned he hid from God. When we sin we would always find our selves hiding from God. However, It does not make good sense, because He knows where we are every minute of the day.

Hence when a person is born and matures, they realize that something is missing in their lives. They may ask as I did, what is there to life? There must be a purpose or reason for my being born? True fulfillment and peace can only be found in Jesus Christ. When we accept Jesus Christ as Savior and Lord the Holy Spirit comes and dwells within us, bringing us back into completeness with God. Men and women look and seek to fill this void in their lives by seeking sexual fulfillment.

Some look to financial success and others other areas in the lives to fill this gap, but to no avail, because this gap can only be filled by the Spirit of God. Man is made up of body soul and spirit. Man is first and foremost a spirit that lives in a body and has a soul. In order for man to be in complete unison with God, man's body and soul must be under the Lordship of Jesus Christ.

One thing one must realize is that the impact of one's sexual instinct is very real. One must never pretend that he or she is all 'spirit' and no 'body', or all "spirit" and 'no soul.' It should be understood that until that day when, in God's own timetable, our body will be redeemed even as our spirits are now. This is because man is first and initially spirit that has a soul and lives in a body.

If for reasons other than personal choice a man or woman has to stay single, God's grace is sufficient to enable that person to exercise the necessary control over his or her sexual desires. When one reads Romans 6:7, it is made clear that the Apostle Paul had struggles and challenges in his body. Paul did not remain single because he had no struggles with his sexual instinct, nor did he remain single just for the sake of remaining single. He remained single because he knew that in his case it was the best way for him to accomplish God's call on his life. He never, however, gave vent to his sexual drive. It was within his power to marry and apparently there was no other reason why he did not marry.

A single person must be alert and avoid scenes and situations where their sexual instinct can be aroused. This is so; because a constant state of desire for the fulfillment of one's sexual appetite can be devastating to a person's spiritual life. Thus, it is foolish to pretend that such desires do not exist or to think oneself invincible in its presence. **There is no allowance for a person to give vent to his or her sexual**

desire outside of marriage. However, for the men and women who have no opportunity to marry, there must be a strong dependence and trust upon God. One must never make sex the ultimate goal in their life.

When young persons reach teenage years, there are many issues going on internally and externally with them, they are no longer children and they are also not adults as yet. There are usually hormonal changes taking place within their bodies and it is at this time that they need some one who could understand them and explain to them what they are going through. They would need strength and courage and the grace of God to stand up through their difficulties and declare Jesus Christ Lord of their lives. It is what they do with their lives at this time that would determine their future. Young people do not spoil your future with engaging in illicit sexual activities. You are called to the kingdom for such a time as this, this is your time, embrace it.

THE UNIQUENESS OF BOTH SEXES
(Both Man and Woman)

God gave man and woman their own individual, unique nature and to each of them it is a glory. The unique desires of each are satisfied differently, the result of God's creative wisdom. The basic differences between the male and the female should be looked at and understood from a Biblical perspective. Many men miss the mark in dealing with a woman because they tend to treat and deal with her as if they are dealing with a man like himself.

In creation, God placed Adam in the Garden of Eden and gave him stewardship over the kingdom of God. God created him in a state of consecrated holiness, without sin and therefore with a perfect mind, body and spirit. Thus Adam could exercise obedience to God's command and name everything on earth that needed to be named. Adam's mind was capable of doing it because it was without the effects of sin. To know what Adam was like in his original manhood, one only need to look at the second Adam, the Lord Jesus Christ in all His humanity.

Given the responsibility of stewardship over the earth,

Adam derived his greatest satisfaction from the reproductive process that God had established for the replenishing of the earth. As steward over the earth, Adam was given the responsibility of overseeing the process of re-creation. His unique nature and desire was basically satisfied in relationship to his stewardship, and the reproductive process in it.

When God made and created Adam, all of humanity was placed within him; this means that every person that was born after Adam, came out of Adam, the first man. That is why women are called wo- man. Women are men that have a womb and the whole of mankind was created as man. They may ask as I did, what is there to life? There must be a purpose or reason for my being born? True fulfillment and peace can only be found in Jesus Christ. When we accept Jesus Christ as Savior and Lord the Holy Spirit comes and dwells within us, bringing us back into completeness with God. Men and women look and seek to fill this void in their lives by sexual fulfillment.

Some look to financial success and others other areas in their lives to fill this gap, but to no avail, because this gap can be filled only by the Spirit of God. Man is made up of body, soul and spirit. Man is first and foremost a spirit that lives in a body and has a soul. In order for man to be in complete unison with God, man's body and soul must be under the Lordship of Jesus Christ.

From then until now it has never changed, man still derives his greatest satisfaction from the reproductive process of his stewardship over the earth.

His job – whether in farming or sales, being a corporate manager, or even more recent a computer specialist – is still where a man finds his basic satisfaction in life.

Men are created that way. God's pattern for the replenishing of the earth through the process of each seed-bearing tree, reproducing after its own kind was then transferred to the reproduction process for mankind.

To replenish the earth, God established a reproductive process whereby the man would be replenished with humanity. Because the reproductive process of replenishing the earth was the most satisfying to a man's unique nature in relation to his job, it became the same in relationship to a woman. The same principle applied to both stewardships – that of the earth and of the family.

Women have been created to nurture and are endowed with a nurturing instinct.

They are the center of the home. Even in this modern day and age when women hold top positions at corporate levels, women are still nurturers. However, they occupy many roles, they are wife, mother, working housewife and caregivers.

THE ANSWER

In my quest I have learnt and have come to understand a number of ways a God fearing Christian person can use to help deal with and keep their sexual desires under control. This answer was achieved after a long process of time and I guarantee anyone if tried, will work for them. A normal person's sexual desire is not something with which to play and take for granted, or even looked at as ungodly. This is something that is in-born and created by God and should be looked at closely. One person's sexual desire may differ from another; one person's sexual desire and drive may be extremely high while another may be low. Hence a suitable solution need to be used and adapted to deal with this particular situation in the lives of both men and women and single persons in particular.

In my life it was a bit difficult at first, because I was married for ten years - I am still relatively young I might add - and so my hormones are still in good working order. However the road to gaining freedom in this area was not a very easy one. I had to deal with it without any literature other than the Word of God. My single friends were not much help either, hence this book.

These are some helpful points that a single person and

even a person whose spouse is not around can endeavor to do in order to keep his/her sexual desires or urges under control. I urge anybody who honestly would like to control this part of his/her life to follow these six steps. God has given us authority in His Word to deal with certain situations, and when we do what He has asked us to do, then He will do the rest, and **God can do anything but fail.**

These points are:

BY A LIFE OF PRAYER

There is power in prayer and prayer changes things. Prayer is essential to the existence of our very being. It is like the water that one pours on a plant for it to grow and bring forth new life. It is through prayer and in our communication with God that we are able to grow and become mature Christians. It is because of this maturity that one would be able to deal effectively with being single and the varied emotions that a single person will experience. My pastor always says that "if you do not pray you would not stay and if you do not fast you would not last" and this is so true in the life of every Christian.

Everyday that you wake up there are battles to be fought in both the spiritual and physical realms, hence these fundamental principles must be applied to a person's life in order to experience a successful and victorious Christian life.

As Christians, every day we face challenges. It is because we are in Christ and know that whatever we may face during the day, we do not have to face by ourselves; but we have the assurance that we are not alone and that we have an advocate on our side - Jesus Christ the Righteous one. He is always interceding on our behalf to the Father.

Prayer is something that must be done not just in the

morning and at night, but throughout the day. Our mind is the battleground where many battles take place, that is why the Scriptures tell us in Prov.4:23 *"Above all else, guard your heart, for it affects everything you do."*(NLT) We are influenced by our senses - seeing, hearing touching, tasting. This is where a person is coerced and usually gets trapped in Satan's web. He disguises himself as an angel of light, but he only comes to steel, kill and destroy, but Christ came that we might have life and have it more abundantly. (Jn.10:10)

When we see and hear we would undoubtedly want to touch, and then if it stays in our minds long enough, we would eventually want to taste and experience what ever we have seen and heard, especially if it looks and sounds very inviting – and sex can be made to look very inviting. This can be done through pornography and illicit sexual activity. Unfortunately, it is only when one has succumbed to one's sexual desires and the act has been completed that remorse steps in. Only too late do they realize that they we were set up, 'big-time' by the devil.

A person can pray while driving or traveling to work or school even while walking in the streets, thus man's excuse of not having time to pray is not realistic, and is really a non-issue. I tell people whom I counsel with all the time that prayer is very simple, that they can talk to God just as they talk to their best friend or me. Praying and talking to God is very simple. God would always meet us where we are.

Prayer is talking and opening our heart to God, just as a person would talk to someone that they know and can see, the same way we can talk to God; the only difference is that we cannot see Him. We can feel His presence and know that He hears and answers prayer, no matter what the circumstances are. When in trouble sometimes all we have to say is "Jesus". There is nothing too hard for God to do for us.

Jesus is our counselor, someone to whom that we can

tell our problems to, when the trials of this life seem to overwhelm us. He would not betray our trust. When we have done things that we believe to be terrible and are ashamed to tell anyone, we can always count on Jesus, for the scriptures tells us that 'He is touched with the feelings of our infirmities' (Heb.4:15) and 'He is a friend that sticketh closer than a brother' (Prov.18:24). He knows our very thoughts and nothing is hid from Him, He is just waiting on us to come to Him, humbling ourselves at His feet and asking for His forgiveness when we sin.

James 4:7 states:

> **"Therefore submit to God, resist the devil and he will flee from you. Draw near to God and He will draw near to you."** vr. 8

When we are in right standing with God He will give us the very desire of our hearts. When our ways please the Lord and we are doing what is right in His sight, He cannot but give us the very desires of our hearts, even if it may be a husband or wife. The Bible states that we should occupy till He comes, hence we must occupy ourselves and do what He has commissioned us to do, until He sends our husband or wife into our lives. When He does, I can assure you that it will be worth the wait.

The Bible also tells us that we should not be to anxious for anything (Phil.4:6). If it is in God's will that we have something, it will always be in time. We need to understand that man's timing and God's timing are not always the same.

I have a friend who once complained to me that she has been single for so long, and that God has not seen it fit to send her a mate. I asked her if she was really ready for her mate, if God sent one for her at that very moment. She was at a loss for an answer. She was not ready, because she still had someone from her past very much in her heart and mind, therefore God could not release any person to come into her life at that time.

Many of us blame God for not sending our "Mister Right" or "Miss Right" into our lives when we are the ones who are hindering God from blessing us with our spouse. We need to pray earnestly and put away all the soul ties that we have had with our previous partners in the spiritual realm, releasing God's hand in order that He can send us the partner whom He has reserved for us. The Bible states that we should pray without ceasing, and when we do this, every decision made in our lives would be in the will of God.

In order to be an over-comer, and have control over our sexual desires prayer is essential. As single people both young and not so young, we need to have and cultivate our relationship with God and *"Let this mind be in you which was in Christ Jesus."*Phil.2: 5 (NKJV) We have a High Priest who was *"in all points tempted as we are, yet with out sin."* Heb.4: 15 He lived a sinless life so can we, because He said that He would not give us more than we could bear, and He would always make a way of escape for us. He is our Savior and our Lord.

BY READING GOD'S WORD DAILY

Reading the Word of God on a daily basis is a necessity for the child of God to live a victorious Christian life. The Bible is the instruction manual for the Christian believer and whatever counsel or direction that we need can be found in it, for the Word of God is a lamp unto our feet and a light unto our path (Ps.119:105), guiding us into the path where we should go.

John 1:vr.1-5

> *"In the beginning the Word already existed. He was with God, and he was God. vr.1*
>
> *He was in the beginning with God vr.2*
>
> *He created everything there is. Nothing exists that he didn't make. vr.3*
>
> *Life itself was in him, and this life gives light to everyone. vr.4*
>
> *The light shines through the darkness, and the darkness can never extinguish it.vr.5 (NLT)*

It is imperative for the Christian believer that the reading and meditating on the Word of God become part of our every day routine. Paul states that the Word of God is quick. The Apostle Paul states in Heb.4:12

> **The Word is full of living power. It is sharper than the sharpest knife, cutting deep into the innermost thoughts and desires. It exposes us to what we really are. (NLT)**

Any direction that we are looking for can be found in the Bible, hence one is without excuse and God would hold us liable for the choices that we make in life.

The Word of God says in John 15:3

> ***You are already clean because of the word which I have spoken to you vr. 3***
>
> ***If you abide in Me, and My works abide you, you will ask what you desire, and it shall be done for you."* vr.7 *(NKJV)***

One can only be made clean when the Word of God is

read and meditated upon, enabling the very substance of God's Word to get deep down into our spirit and take root in our hearts and minds, making an indelible change in our lives. When this happens, then the wrong things that we did and said, we would not be able to do them any more, because of the convicting and controlling power of God in our lives. The Word of God states in James 1:21: -

James 1:21:
"Therefore lay aside all filthiness and overflow of wickedness, and receive with meekness the implanted Word, which is able to save your souls" (NKJV)

The Word of God is power and it is life and should not be taken lightly.

James 1:12:
"Blessed is the man who endures temptation; for when he has been approved, he will receive the crown of life which the Lord has promised to those who love Him."vr.12
Let no one say when he is tempted, "I am tempted by God", for God cannot be tempted with evil, nor does He Himself tempt anyone **vr.13**
But each one is tempted when he is drawn away by his own desires and enticed. **vr.14**
Then, when desire has conceived, it gives birth to sin; and sin when it is full-grown, brings forth death. **vr.15** *(NLT)*

The devil would use any tactic that he can to get to our minds to distort our thoughts. However, the Apostle Paul in

Phil. 4:8 admonishes us to: -

> *"Fix your thoughts on what is true and honorable and right. Think about things that are pure and lovely and admirable. Think about things that are excellent and worthy of praise (NLT).*

The psalmist David who was a man after God's heart wrote these words in Psalm 130:5 to the Lord

> *I am counting on the Lord; yes, I am counting on him. I have put my hope in his word .vr.5*
> *long for the Lord, More than sentries long for the dawn, Yes, more than sentries long for the dawn.vr.6 (NLT)*

BY KEEPING BUSY AND ESPECIALLY BUSY IN THE SERVICE OF GOD.

Keeping busy especially in the things of God, is one of the ways in which a single person keeps focused. Keeping busy is one of the major methods that I have used and that has been very successful for me. I have a full time job, and am very active in the church that I attend; also I now live with my parents who are not experiencing the best of health, thereby leaving little room for anything else. I am always occupied. Therefore, there is little time for me to dwell and meditate on my sexual urges or feelings whenever they arise.

There are ministries in the church that you attend and can get involved in. Tell your pastor that you would like to become involved in ministry in the church. If you are faithful to the particular ministry that has been assigned to you, then God would increase your ministry. God never fails. What ever you give to God He will always multiplies it back unto you. We just have to know from whom our strength comes, and it is not from our selves, but our strength and abilities comes from God. I have gone through the process and have learnt that there is nothing like 'can't', because there is nothing impossible with God. Faithfulness to God would always be rewarded.

ALWAYS REMEMBER AND FOCUS ON THE PROMISES THAT GOD HAS MADE TO US, BOTH PERSONALLY AND THROUGH HIS WORD

The Word of God is filled with many promises that we as believers need to keep very close to our hearts and minds. God has made certain promises to us as believers, that we need to act upon. One of these promises is that no weapon that is formed against us shall prosper (Isaiah. 54:17). He never said that weapons would not be formed, but that it shall not prosper. Another promise is that there are no temptations know unto man ... but with every temptation He will make a way of escape. (1 Cor.10:13)

God also gives us promises through the Word of God, words of prophecy and also ministering directly to us. Most prophecies are usually confirmation of what God has already ministered to us. Prophecies also speak things into our lives that we cannot conceive, and what God has ordained for us since the very beginning of time, we may believe that it is impossible, but as long as we stay in Christ and follow the path that He has ordained for us, then we will see what He has ordained come to pass in our lives.

REMEMBER ALL THE PROMISES AND COMMITMENT THAT WE IN TURN HAVE MADE TO HIM

If one is still experiencing serious falls into sin, then serious prayer and fasting should be done in order to "bring the flesh under subjection".

Single persons who are 'Born Again Christians' should take a 'vow of Abstinence'. Taking a vow of abstinence is not for weak persons, because it takes a strong person to stand up and declare to anyone that they have taken a vow of abstinence; keeping themselves chaste and pure before God; that they have decided to leave sexual activity for when they are married on their wedding night when they come together as husband and wife for the first time.

Some of the promises that should be made are: -

- Say no to premarital sex.
- No to dating unsaved persons.
- Reading God's Word daily.
- Praying daily.
- Making sure you are appropriately dressed before leaving home.
- To be obedient to those in authority.
- Shun the very appearance of evil.

It is only through one's love for God can victory over the flesh be experienced.

This I know without a shadow of a doubt. These points would help the single believer become an overcomer and be victorious over sexual desires. Sexual desires are not sinful. It is part of our nature that we were born with. Copulation, the coming together of man and woman in sexual union, should only be exercised within the confines of marriage. Outside of that it is sin.

THINK OF GOD'S LOVE FOR US, AND OUR LOVE FOR HIM.

John, the beloved of Jesus and who was always close to Him and was part of His inner circle, spoke about God's deep love for us in John 3:16. He stated that God loved the world so much that He gave His only beloved Son, so that anyone who believes in Him may not die but have eternal life.

God's purpose for our lives is that we allow Him to make his home and abode in us, that is to take up permanent residence in our lives. This can only be done through God and the shed blood of Jesus. He wants us to have our roots and foundation embedded in love so that we may have the power to understand how broad and long, how high and deep Christ's love is for us.

If we truly love Him, then we would not want to do anything that would displease or embarrass Him. This is the main reason why we need to live a chaste life. If we love Him, like a good lover, we would want Him around all the time and do whosoever is pleasing in His sight. Sexual sin would never be an option.

THE JOY OF BEING SINGLE

When Adam was alone in the Garden of Eden he was quite busy and contented, because he enjoyed what he did. In Genesis 2:15 the Word of God states that God *"put him in the Garden of Eden to dress it and keep it."* Adam did not feel lonely and dejected but was happy doing what he was commanded to do. So too, we that are single should be happy in our present station in life and endeavor to do our best for God in our singleness. When we are busy doing God's work then God would have no choice but to get busy on our behalf. He said in His Word that **no good thing** He would withhold from them that love Him and walk uprightly. Single people should be very happy people.

From a single woman's point of view, there is no husband around to cook and do laundries for. The only laundry that you may have to do is your own, or your children's if you have. I never realized this blessing until I became single. Don't get me wrong; I did it when I was married. I enjoyed doing the cooking because I love to cook and bake and feel very much at home when I am in the kitchen. However, it was shortly after I became single that it slowly and amazingly dawned upon me that I did not have to cook and do other household chores if I did not want to because my husband was no longer at home. I also did not have any children to prepare meals for and to take care of, so I more or less was placed into the position of doing whatever I fancied in that area.

To give you a hint of what I ate at home for a couple of years. I will let you in on my very own private grocery list, please do not be jealous, and do not tell anyone. My groceries consisted of different brands of cornflakes, wholegrain cereal and milk, along with fruits and fresh vegetables in case I wanted to make a salad. I hardly ever cooked because I ate out during the day, so there was no need for serious cooking at night, when I reached home. Hence cereals!

This period of my life suddenly came to an end when I moved back piece-by-piece to my parents' home because my mother became ill and I was needed there. When she became ill she stayed with me for a few months, and when the Christmas season came she expressed her desire to return to her home. My lifestyle has now changed again. They love and enjoy having me home with them again. It was a big adjustment for me at first; nevertheless I am happy and very contented with my life at present.

I achieved many of my life's goals at this particular stage in my life and have turned my trials into successes. If I can do it so can you. God is able to do abundantly above all that we could ever ask or think, and only He, knows what our tomorrows will be. When situations happen to us that we may not understand, we just have to trust and hope in God, putting ourselves into His mighty hand. His hand is never too small to hold us, and He would never let us fall. I know that without a shadow of doubt, because I have experienced His goodness and His mercies over and over and over. There can be no genuine testimony without a test.

The only thing that I have missed is the friendship that my ex husband and I had and the sex; I have to mention this because it is a vital part of any marriage. I am now happy and free and I am what I am because of the many trials and experiences that I have gone through. It is something that all 'Born again Christians' must go through, in order to come out as fine/pure gold. We can rest assured that He will never give us more than we can bear. When we are going through we may find it hard, but just hold on, morning will come and our blessings and rewards along with it. We need not holler and moan about our situation and what we have been through and what we are currently experiencing. God had to have trusted us enough, to allow whatever the trial and challenges we go through in our daily lives, to take place.

The Word of God states that He will not give us more than we can bear and Satan the accuser of the brethren always has to get permission from God in order to touch us in any area of our lives. Like Job, God is only setting us up for a blessing, whereby our place of pain becomes our place of gain.

Probably the most complete illustration of God's attitude towards expressions of sexual love – marital love - is in the Old Testament, in the Song of Solomon. For centuries Christians have used this book as an allegory of Christ (the Bridegroom) and His Church (His Bride). It is valid to say that the Song of Solomon presents a good picture of Christ and His Church, but is also primarily speaking of a love relationship between husband and wife.

One of the primary purposes of the Song of Solomon is to present God's perspective on sexual love, and this love is only recognized within the bounds of holy matrimony. The book is highly intimate and yet it is set against an ethical/moral background of monogamy and premarital chastity. The Song of Solomon speaks definitively that sex in marriage is pure before God, and that any kind of sexual love between husband and wife is holy and beautiful before God.

THE SONG OF SOLOMON

Saturated with stories of sexual escapades, secret rendezvous, and extramarital affairs, today's media teach that immorality means freedom, perversion is natural, and commitment is old fashion. However, sexual intercourse, the physical and emotional union of male and female, should be a holy means of celebrating love, producing children, and experiencing pleasure, protected by the commitment of marriage. God thinks that sex is important, and Scripture contains numerous guidelines for its use and warnings of its misuse.

Song of Solomon highlights the love relationship between a man and a woman, their love, courtship and marriage. It is a moving story, drama, and poem, featuring the love dialogue between a simple Jewish maiden (the young woman) and her lover (Solomon, the king). In it they describe intimate details of their feelings for each other and their longings to be together. Throughout the dialogue, sex, and marriage are put in their proper, God given perspective.

There are two levels of love that can be learnt from Song of Solomon. The first one teaches about love, marriage and sex; the other, about God's overwhelming love for his people.

I included this book of the Bible so that young men and women can glimpse how beautiful, wonderful and pure love relationship in Christ can be, when done according to the principles of God. As you read Song of Solomon, remember that you are loved by God, and commit yourself to seeing life, sex and marriage from His viewpoint. Young men and women, it is worth the wait. Give it all you've got, and let God do the rest. When you do this, you will never go wrong. You are truly blessed.

The Song of Songs

This *Song of Songs, more wonderful than any other,* **was** *composed by King Solomon*

The Wedding Day

Young Woman: "Kiss me again and again, for your love is sweeter than wine. How fragrant your cologne, and how great your name! No wonder all the young girls love you! Take me with you; come let's run!

The King has brought me into his palace. How happy we will be! Your love is better than wine. No wonder all the girls love you!

I am dark but beautiful, O girls of Jerusalem, tanned as the dark tents of Kadar."

King Solomon: "But lovely as the silken tents of Solomon!"

Young Woman: "Don't look down on me, you city girls, just because my complexion is so dark—the sun has tanned me. My brothers were angry with me and sent me out into the sun to tend the vineyards, but see what it has done to me! Tell me, O one I love, where are you leading your flock today? Where will you be at noon? For I will come and join you there instead of wandering like a vagabond among the flocks of your companions."

King Solomon: "If you don't know, O most beautiful woman in all the world, follow the trail of my flock to the shepherds' tents, and there feed your sheep and their lambs. What a lovely filly you are, my love! How lovely your cheeks are, with your hair falling down upon them! How stately your neck with that long string of jewels. We shall make you golden earrings and silver beads."

Young Woman: "The king lies on his bed, enchanted by the fragrance of my perfume. My beloved one is a sachet of myrrh lying between my breasts."

King Solomon: "My beloved is a bouquet of flowers in the gardens of Engedi. How beautiful you are, my love, how beautiful! Your eyes are soft as doves'. What a lovely, pleasant thing you are, lying here upon the grass, shaded by the cedar trees and firs."

Young Woman: "I am the rose of Sharon, the lily of the valley."

King Solomon: "Yes, a lily among thorns, so is my beloved as compared with any other girls."

The Girl: "My lover is an apple tree, the finest in the orchard as compared with any of the other youths. I am seated in his much-desired shade and his fruit is lovely to eat. He brings me to the banquet hall and everyone can see how much he loves me. Oh, feed me with your love— your 'raisins' and your 'apples'—for I am utterly lovesick. His left hand is under my head and with his right hand he embraces me. O girls of Jerusalem, I adjure you by the gazelles and deer in the park, that you do not awaken my lover. Let him sleep.

Memories of Courtship

Ah, I hear him—my beloved! Here he comes, leaping upon the mountains and bounding over the hills. My beloved is like a gazelle or young deer. Look, there he is behind the wall, now looking in at the windows.

My beloved said to me, 'Rise up, my love, my fair one, and come away. For the winter is past, the rain is over and gone. The flowers are springing up and the time of the singing of birds has come. Yes, spring is here. The leaves are coming out and the grape vines are in blossom. How delicious they smell! Arise, my love, my fair one, and come away.

My dove is hiding behind some rocks, behind an outcrop of the cliff. Call to me and let me hear your lovely voice and see your handsome face.

The little foxes are ruining the vineyards. Catch them, for the grapes are all in blossom.

My beloved is mine and I am his. He is feeding among the lilies! Before the dawn comes and the shadows flee away, come to me, my beloved, and be like a gazelle or a young stag on the mountains of spices.

One night my lover was missing from my bed. I got up to look for him but couldn't find him. I went out into the streets of the city and the roads to seek him, but I searched in vain. The police stopped me and I said to them, 'Have you seen him anywhere, this one I love so much?' It was only a little while afterwards that I found him and held him and would not let him go until I had brought him into my childhood home, into my mother's old bedroom. I adjure you, O women of Jerusalem by the gazelles and deer of the park, not to awake my lover. Let him sleep."

Memories of Engagement

The Young Women of Jerusalem: "Who is this sweeping in from the deserts like a cloud of smoke along the ground, smelling of myrrh and frankincense and every other spice that can be bought? Look, it is the chariot of Solomon with sixty of the mightiest men of his army surrounding it. They are all skilled swordsmen and experienced bodyguards. Each one has his sword upon his thigh to defend his king against any onslaught in the night. For King Solomon made himself a chariot from the wood of Lebanon. Its posts are silver, its canopy gold, the seat is purple; and the back is inlaid with these words: 'With love from the girls of Jerusalem!' "

Young Woman: "Go out and see King Solomon, O young women of Zion; see the crown with which his mother crowned him on his wedding day, his day of gladness."

King Solomon: "How beautiful you are, my love, how beautiful! Your eyes are those of doves. Your hair falls across your face like flocks of goats that frisk across the slopes of Gilead. Your teeth are white as sheep's wool, newly shorn and washed; perfectly matched, without one missing. Your lips are like a thread of scarlet—and how beautiful your mouth. Your cheeks are matched loveliness behind your locks. Your neck is stately as the tower of David, jeweled with a thousand heroes' shields. Your breasts are like twin fawns of a gazelle, feeding among the lilies. Until the morning dawns and the shadows flee away, I will go to the mountain of myrrh and to the hill of frankincense. You are so beautiful, my love, in every part of you.

Come with me from Lebanon, my bride. We will look down from the summit of the mountain, from the top of Mount Hermon, where the lions have their dens, and panthers prowl. You have ravished my heart, my lovely one, my bride; I am overcome by one glance of your eyes, by a single bead of your necklace. How sweet is your love, my darling, my bride. How much better it is than mere wine. The perfume of your love is more fragrant than all the richest spices. Your lips, my dear, are made of honey. Yes, honey and cream are under your tongue, and the scent of your garments is like the scent of the mountains and cedars of Lebanon.

My darling bride is like a private garden, a spring that no one else can have, a fountain of my own. You are like a lovely orchard bearing precious fruit, with the rarest of perfumes; nard and saffron, calamus and cinnamon, and perfume from every other incense tree, as well as myrrh and aloes, and every other lovely spice. You are a garden fountain, a well of living water, refreshing as the streams from the Lebanon mountains."

Young Woman: "Come, north wind, awaken; come, south wind, blow upon my garden and waft its lovely perfume to my beloved. Let him come into his garden and eat its choicest fruits."

King Solomon: "I am here in my garden, my darling, my bride! I gather my myrrh with my spices and eat my honeycomb with my honey. I drink my wine with my milk."

The Young Women of Jerusalem: "Oh, lover and beloved, eat and drink!   Yes, drink deeply!"

Young Woman: "One night as I was sleeping, my heart awakened in a dream. I heard the voice of my beloved; he was knocking at my bedroom door. 'Open to me, my darling, my lover, my lovely dove,' he said, 'for I have been out in the night and am covered with dew.'

But I said, 'I have disrobed. Shall I get dressed again? I have washed my feet, and should I get them soiled?'

My beloved tried to unlatch the door and my heart was moved for him. I jumped up to open it and my hands dripped with perfume, my fingers with lovely myrrh as I pulled back the bolt. I opened to my beloved, but he was gone. My heart stopped. I searched for him but couldn't find him anywhere. I called to him, but there was no reply. The guards found me and struck and wounded me. The watchman on the wall tore off my veil. I adjure, O women of Jerusalem, if you find my beloved one, tell him that I am sick with love."

The Young Women of Jerusalem: "O woman of rare beauty, what is it about your loved one that is better than any other, that you command us this?"

Young Woman: "My beloved one is tanned and handsome, better than ten thousand others! His head is purest gold, and he has wavy, raven hair. His eyes are like doves beside the water brooks, deep and quiet. His cheeks are like sweetly scented beds of spices. His lips are perfume lilies, his breath like myrrh. His arms are round bars of gold set with topaz; his body is bright ivory encrusted with jewels. His legs are, as pillars of marble set in sockets of finest gold, like cedars of Lebanon; none can rival him. His mouth is altogether sweet, lovable in every way. Such, O women of Jerusalem, is my beloved, my friend."

The Young Women of Jerusalem: "O rarest of beautiful women, where has your loved one gone? We will help you find him."

Young Woman: "He has gone down to his garden, to his spice beds, to pasture his flock and to gather the lilies. I am my beloved's and my beloved is mine. He pastures his flock among the lilies!"

Praising the Bride's Beauty

King Solomon: "O my beloved, you are as beautiful as the lovely land of Tirzah, yes, beautiful as Jerusalem, and how you capture my heart. Look the other way, for your eyes have overcome me! Your hair, as it falls across your face, is like a flock of goats frisking down the slopes of Gilead. Your teeth are white as freshly washed ewes, perfectly matched and not one missing. Your cheeks are matched loveliness behind your hair. I have sixty other wives, all queens, and eighty concubines, and unnumbered virgins available to me; but you, my dove, my perfect one, are the only one among them all, without an equal! The women of Jerusalem were delighted when they saw you and even the queens and concubines praise you. 'Who is this,' they ask, 'arising as the dawn, fair as the moon, pure as the sun, so utterly captivating.' "

Young Woman: "I went down into the orchard of nuts and out to the valley to see the springtime there, to see whether the grape vines were budding or the pomegranates were blossoming yet. Before I realized it I was stricken with terrible homesickness and wanted to be back among my own people."

The Young Women of Jerusalem: "Return, return to us, O maid of Shulam. Come back, come back, that we may see you once again."

Young Woman: "Why should you seek a mere Shulammite?"

King Solomon: "Because you dance so beautifully. How beautiful your tripping feet, O queenly maiden. Your rounded thighs are like jewels, the work of the most skilled of craftsmen. Your navel is lovely as a goblet filled with wine. Your waist is like a heap of wheat set about with lilies. Your two breasts are like two fawns, yes, lovely twins. Your neck is stately as an ivory tower, your eyes as limpid pools in Heshbon by the gate of Bath-rabbim. Your nose is shapely like the tower of Lebanon overlooking Damascus.

As Mount Carmel crowns the mountains, so your hair is your crown. The king is held captive in your queenly tresses.

Oh, how delightful you are; how pleasant, O love, for utter delight! You are tall and slim like a palm tree, and your breasts are like its clusters of dates. I said, I will climb up into the palm tree and take hold of its branches. Now may your breasts be like grape clusters, and the scent of your breath like apples, and your kisses as exciting as the best of wine, smooth and sweet, causing the lips of those who are asleep to speak."
The Girl: "I am my beloved's and I am the one he desires. Come, my beloved, let us go out into the fields and stay in the villages. Let us get up early and go out to the vineyards and see whether the vines have budded and whether the blossoms have opened and whether the pomegranates are in flower. And there I will give you my love. There the mandrakes give forth their fragrance and the rarest fruits are at our doors, the new as well as old, for I have stored them up
For my beloved.

Oh, if only you were my brother; then I could kiss you no matter who was watching, and no one would laugh at me. I would bring you to my childhood home, and there you would teach me. I would give you spiced wine to drink, sweet pomegranate wine. His left hand would be under my head and his right hand would embrace me, I adjure you, O women of Jerusalem, not to awaken him until he please."

The Young Women of Jerusalem: "Who is this coming up from the desert, leaning on her beloved?"

King Solomon: "Under the apple trees where your mother gave birth to you in her travail, there I awakened your love."

The Girl: "Seal me in your heart with permanent betrothal, for love is strong as death and jealousy is as cruel as Sheol. It flashes fire, the very flame of Jehovah. Many waters cannot quench the flame of love; neither can the floods drown it. If a man tried to buy it with everything he owned, he couldn't do it. We have a little sister too young for breasts. What shall we do if someone asks to marry her?"

King Solomon: "If she has no breasts we will build upon her a battlement of silver, and if she is a door we will enclose her with cedar boards."

The Girl: "I am slim, tall, and full-breasted and I have found favor in my lover's eyes. Solomon had a vineyard at Baal-hamon which he rented out to some farmers there, the rent being one thousand pieces of silver from each. But as for my own vineyard, you, O Solomon, shall have my thousand pieces of silver and I will give two hundred pieces to those who care for it.

O my beloved, living in the gardens, how wonderful that your companions may listen to your voice; let me hear it too. Come quickly, my beloved, and be like a gazelle or young deer upon the mountains of spices."

A PLEDGE OF ABSTINENCE

On this date, _____, I am choosing to abstain from all sexual activity until I am married.

Whether I 've had sex or not, from this day forward, I will use self-control in my relationships and save myself for the special person that I will marry.

signed

_____

CONGRATULATIONS

Congratulations, you have just made a quality decision which should be very proud of

_____

CONTACT INFORMATION

Dr. Barbara John
Mercer Road
Diego Martin
Trinidad
West Indies

Email Address: ChristianCounseling@drbarbarajohn.com
Website: www.drbarbarajohn.net

REFERENCES

The Oxford English Dictionary. The Fifth Edition

The Living Bible. Published by Tyndale House Publishers. Illinois.

The Holy Bible KJV. World Bible Publishers. Iowa Falls, Iowa

Lovematters.com/startover.htm

Life Application Study Bible. NLT. Tyndale House Publishers, Inc. Illinois.

Most of the quotes were taken for the Life Application Study Bible in order to bring more enlightenment of the scriptures to the young readers.

Ingram Content Group UK Ltd.
Milton Keynes UK
UKHW012049220623
423898UK00001B/155